D0281396

LEARNING MENTORS IN SCHOOLS
POLICY AND PRACTICE

Leora Cruddas

Trentham Books

Stoke on Trent, UK and Sterling, USA

Trentham Books Limited
Westview House   22883 Quicksilver Drive
734 London Road   Sterling
Oakhill   VA 20166-2012
Stoke on Trent   USA
Staffordshire
England ST4 5NP

© 2005 Leora Cruddas

All rights reserved. No part of this publication may be reproduced or transmitted
in any form or by any means, electronic or mechanical including photocopying, recording or any information storage or retrieval system, without prior permission in writing from the publishers.

First published 2005

M10 3067

British Library Cataloguing-in-Publication Data
A catalogue record for this book is available from the British Library

ISBN-13: 978-1-85856-331-2
ISBN-10: 1-85856-331-3

EduAction is a new organisation created to deliver key services of the highest quality to the schools in the London Borough of Waltham Forest. The views expressed in this book are the author's and do not necessarily reflect those of EduAction (Waltham Forest) Ltd.

The image on the front cover is detail from a mural documenting children's experiences and journey through their primary school life, from reception to Year 6. The mural was created by the Art Club at Hillyfield Primary School, but primarily by young artist Krunal Tailor. It formed part of the 2004 exhibition: *Transitions – children's art about change*, at the Changing Rooms Gallery in Lloyd Park, Waltham Forest, which showcased work done by young people with their learning mentors in Waltham Forest schools. The cover image is reproduced with the kind permission of Steve Lancashire, Headteacher at Hillyfield Primary School.

Designed and typeset by Trentham Print Design Ltd, Chester and printed in Great Britain by Alden Group Ltd, Oxford.

Dedication

*To Sandy Posnikoff, my friend, colleague and 'dialogue partner'
in the process of writing this book. I dedicate this to you in
celebration of a very happy collaboration.*

*And to learning mentors everywhere and the children and
young people with whom they work.*

CONTENTS

Acknowledgements • ix

List of case study contributors • xi

Abbreviations • xiii

Chapter 1
Introduction • 1

PART ONE
POLICY AND SCHOOL IMPROVEMENT

Chapter 2
Learning mentors in the policy context • 15

Chapter 3
Redefining school improvement – the challenge
to school leaders • 35

Chapter 4
Managing learning mentor provision • 51

PART TWO
TOWARDS A THEORY-BASED MODEL OF
LEARNING MENTORING

Chapter 5
A functional definition of learning mentor practice –
towards person-centred practice • 73

Chapter 6
Theoretical anchors: Learning from theoretical
models informing practice in the
international context • 83

Chapter 7
Towards a model of learning mentoring • 93

PART THREE
PRACTICE-BASED EVIDENCE

Chapter 8
Developing and maintaining supportive
mentoring relationships • 111

Chapter 9
Learning mentoring: a complementary service • 151

Chapter 10
Working within an extended range of networks • 183

Parting thoughts: seizing opportunities in a
climate of possibility • 201

Appendix A • 203

References • 205

Index • 209

Acknowledgements

I would like to express my thanks to those who supported me during the writing of this book. I owe an enormous debt to the learning mentors and strand-co-ordinators who contributed case studies. The richness and variety of the material they provided is the real strength of this book. I want to mention particularly the learning mentors, line managers and headteachers in Waltham Forest schools, with whom I have had the great pleasure and privilege of working.

I want to record very special thanks to Sandy Posnikoff, to whom this book is dedicated. She combined just the right amount of critical engagement with my ideas, with generous support while I was writing. Thank you also to Leanne Rose-Slade in Canada, who read chapters one and two, and gave me valuable feedback on my presentation of Child and Youth Care work in North America. And thanks to Hazel Abbott who read an early draft with her headteacher's hat on and provided useful comments.

My colleagues in the pan-London learning mentor strand co-ordinators' forum have provided a constant source of support and challenge over the years. A special thanks to Jimmy Nwaogwugwu who was my 'mentor' when I first came to post, and whose clear-sightedness still challenges and inspires me. I also want to mention two other learning mentor strand co-ordinator colleagues who, in different ways, have both challenged and inspired me: Chris Davison and Nikki Daniel, with whom I have shared many hours of valuable debate about learning mentoring.

Thanks too, to Michael Fielding, whose ideas have influenced much of my thinking in recent years. Many of his ideas permeate the pages of this book. I remain in awe of Michael's huge intellect, matched by his commitment to social justice in education. Similarly, Helen Colley's work has challenged and influenced my thinking and writing.

I am very grateful to my manager, Geoff Headley, who has been a constant source of strength, support and encouragement, and who has been generous with his time in reading the manuscript for this book. I am also grateful to my team of colleagues in Excellence in Cities, particularly to Sarah Johnson, my colleague and friend, whose dedication to learning mentoring and young people is inspiring, and who produced two case studies for this book at very short notice. Thanks also to Kate Honeyford who helped me overcome my fear of data and taught me what jagged profiles are. I would like to express my thanks to the senior managers of EduAction (Waltham Forest), particularly Eleanor Schooling, for giving me permission to write this book.

Thanks also, to colleagues at Trentham Books, particularly to Gillian Klein for believing in this book and for the hours of careful editing.

Finally, to my partner, Peter Rapp, whose love and support have given me the courage and the domestic space to write.

List of case study contributors

1. Angela Struthers (Whittingham Community School)
2. Andrew Morris (Greenleaf Primary School)
3. Pat Smith (George Mitchell School)
4. Sandy Posnikoff (CEA @ Islington)
5. Jennifer Slocombe (Newington Green Primary School)
6. Veronica Gyamerah and Jasbir Phull (Davies Lane Primary School)
7. Wilma Dominque (Leytonstone School)
8. Kris Black and Sarah Edwards (Cann Hall Primary)
9. Julie Smith and Denise Curtis (Henry Maynard Infant School)
10. Diane Thomas (Sybourn Junior School)
11. Su Clark (Barclay Junior School)
12. Sally Barlow (Coppermill Primary)
13. Lesley Bolle (Highams Park)
14. Su Monro (Whitehall Primary School)
15. Vevi Constantinedes (Walthamstow School for Girls)
16. Sue Millard (Thomas Gamuel Primary School) and Diane Thomas (Sybourn Junior School)
17. Tracy D'Vaz (Chingford Hall Primary School)
18. Maggie Ryan (CEA @ Islington)
19. Julie Smith and Denise Curtis (Henry Maynard Infant School)
20. Sarah Johnson (Tom Hood)

21. Annette Collier (Mission Grove Primary School)

22. Andrew Morris (Greenleaf Primary School)

23. Cath Hawley (Worth Valley Primary School)

24. Azziz Mohamed (Warwick School for Boys)

25. Diane Thomas (Sybourn Junior School)

26. Julie Smith and Denise Curtis (Henry Maynard Infant School)

27. Pat Warbrick (St Margaret of Antioch's Primary School)

28. Azziz Mohamed (Warwick School for Boys)

29. Sylvia McLean (Norlington School for Boys)

30. Margaret Cannell (Chingford Foundation School)

31. Sarah Johnson (Tom Hood)

32. Vevi Constantinedes (Walthamstow School for Girls)

33. Angela Rousseau and Margaret Doran (Seven Sisters Primary School)

34. Lesley Bolle (Highams Park Secondary School), Margaret Cannell (Chingford Foundation School), Sylvia McLean (Norlington School for Boys), Sharon Phillip (Willowfield Secondary School) and Leora Cruddas (EduAction)

35. Elizabeth Scott (Camden LEA)

Note – all names of children are pseudonyms and in some cases detail has been changed to protect their identities

Abbreviations

ACYCP	American Association for Child and Youth Care Practice
CRE	Commission for Racial Equality
CSIE	Centre for Studies for Inclusive Education
DfEE:	Department for Education and Employment
DfES	Department for Education and Skills
EAZ	Education Action Zone
EiC	Excellence in Cities
ENTO	The Employment National Training Organisation
GCSE	General Certificate of Secondary Education
ICT	Information and Communication Technology
INSET	In-service training
LEA	Local Education Authority
LM	Learning mentor
NACP	North American Certification Project
NFER	National Foundation for Educational Research
NOS	National Occupational Standards
OECD	Organisation for Economic Co-operation and Development
Ofsted	Office for standards in education
PISA	Programme for International Student Assessment
PSHE	Personal, Social and Health Education
QCA	Qualifications and Curriculum Authority
SATs	Standardised Assessment Tests
SEN	Special Educational Needs
SENJIT	Special Educational Needs Joint Initiative in Training
TOPSS	Training Organisation for Personal Social Services
UNESCO	United Nations Educational, Scientific and Cultural Organisation

1
Introduction

This book documents some of what we know about learning mentor practice. The 35 case studies describe a range of interventions and initiatives that have improved the learning and school experience of children and young people. The practice described is mapped to an existing set of learning mentor functions and positioned by the case studies I have selected. This indicates my own political and ideological beliefs and locates the examination of learning mentor practice within a political frame.

Michael Fielding (2004) analyses the political dimensions of pupil voice work, linking it to what he calls the 'renewal of civic society'. He uses three broad 'standpoints': neo-liberal, emancipatory and post-structuralist, to support his analysis. I use Fielding's taxonomy to develop a broad-brush analysis of how learning mentor practice can be positioned in each of these three standpoints, so as to locate learning mentors within a broader political 'field' (in Bourdieu's terms). I hope this book will engender a constructive and lively dialogue – and the beginning of a body of knowledge.

The difficulties and dangers of neo-liberalism
The neo-liberal position is very close to conservative politics. It attempts to re-write conservative ideals in more publicly

acceptable ways. Thus, from a conservative standpoint, some children, young people and their families lack the personal resources to engage profitably in education or behave in pro-social ways. This is re-written by the neo-liberals as a discourse of 'risk'. Government policies thus appear to be moving away from deficit constructions towards identifying categories of risk. DfEE Circular 10/99 *Social Inclusion: pupil support* identifies a number of groups 'at particular risk'. As Bradford (2000) has noted, constructing certain groups as 'at risk' identifies them as an essentially problematic social category requiring intervention.

Discourses of risk coincide with the rise of what Chris Grey (2001) calls the discourse of learning, in which it is assumed that formal learning is the way out of 'risk'. Fielding writes about the neo-liberal position:

> Its still dominant script is one which invites us to move away from the traditional areas of pastoral and wider engagement with young people and focus more insistently on formal learning in classrooms in school. It is proclamatory, even proud, in its confidence and its insistence that we return again and again to learning. (2004: 203)

It may be difficult on first reading to understand why the tone of this extract appears to take a position *against* learning. Grey has undertaken an astute analysis of the 'learning discourse' in his paper 'Against Learning' (2001). He argues that the learning discourse is 'enmeshed within a largely covert agenda, especially in education policy, which individualises and instrumentalises learning' (Grey, 2001: 2). He interrogates what is meant by the term 'learning' and argues that it is relentlessly performative and directed towards the achievement of a particular set of narrowly prescribed outcomes. Significantly, Grey asserts that part of the learning discourse is the way in which it creates and legitimates certain 'self-responsibilised subject positions' (2001: 7). In other words, these outcomes increasingly also prescribe 'normative' ways of being and behaving.

Colley (2003) observes that if mentoring is centred on 'fixing deficits and reforming deviance' it is merely a way of imposing normative value systems on children and young people.

The 'traditional areas of pastoral and wider engagement with young people' (in the extract above) are co-opted into what Fielding calls the 'well-being' agenda – circle time, mentoring, coaching etc. Fielding acknowledges that at first, this appears to be contradictory. However, he proposes that circle time, mentoring and coaching 'are legitimated as the active sites of emotional intelligence and consequently more sustained engagement in what is seen as the core work of the school i.e. to raise standards of attainment in publicly measurable ways' (Fielding, 2004: 205). In this sense, the social role of education is firmly linked to performance. I will return to education as social practice in the second part of this book and present theories that seek to reintroduce variety, heterodoxy and equality into education.

Learning mentors are very much part of the 'well-being' agenda but they also actively support children and young people's learning. Within neo-liberalism there is the danger that learning mentors will become merely the agents of the standards agenda and engage in purely instrumental practices that can be measured in quantifiable ways. There is also a risk that learning mentors will become the instruments to impose institutional goals on young people in ways that are experienced by them as diminishing and destructive rather than engaging and enabling. If they function within a neo-liberal perspective, there is the danger that learning mentors will be disciplinary agents, who aim to increase compliance among young people whose attitudes and behaviours are perceived as a 'threat' to school improvement.

The limitations of an emancipatory position

At the other end of the political spectrum is the emancipatory position. According to Aronowitz and Giroux: 'The crisis in education is not about the background information that young people allegedly lack, or the inability of students to communicate in order to adapt more readily to the dictates of the dominant culture' (1991: 45), rather it is a crisis framed at the intersections of knowledge, power and culture. The body of radical and emancipatory research on culture and schooling which has emerged in the last twenty years argues that schools are social and cultural institutions where young people are introduced to particular ways of life, where subjectivities are produced, where ways of being-in-the-world are constructed and given legitimacy, or refused and degraded.

James Gee's socio-linguistic theory, supports a view that disenfranchised young people experience a mismatch between their home-based or primary discourse and their school-based or secondary discourse. According to Gee:

> Discourses are ways of being in the world, or forms of life which integrate words, acts, values, beliefs, attitudes, social identities, as well as gestures, glances, body positions and clothes. A Discourse is a sort of 'identity kit' which comes complete with the appropriate costume and instructions on how to act, talk and often write, so as to take on a particular social role. (Gee,1990:142)

Successful pupils' acquisition of the school-based discourse is facilitated by the close match between their primary and secondary discourses: they have had early practice in the home which provides constant support to the school-based discourse and they therefore feel less conflict.

Gee argues:

> Another way to look at discourses is that they are always ways of displaying (through words, actions, values and beliefs) membership of a particular social group or social network (people who associate with each other around a common set of interests goals and activities). (1990:142-3)

Discursive positions are therefore governed by a tacit set of rules about who belongs and who does not, and how we ought to behave. These rules often contradict each other and result in a crisis of choice for the young person between the primary and secondary discourse.

The crises experienced by young people are often encoded in their behaviours. 'Acting out' is a crucial signifier of crisis enacted in the cultural codes of an oppositional discourse: non-standard, 'aggressive' language, oppositional modes of dress, challenging behaviours, rejection of forms of academic knowledge and even literacy. Gee calls this the borderland discourse. The borderland is an 'off-line', peer-based discursive space situated between the home-based or primary discourse and school-based or secondary discourse. The borderland comprises 'a whole set of social practices... and these practices involve not just ways of talking, acting and valuing, but also ways of reading and writing' (Gee, 1990:183). While some pupils successfully negotiate among primary, secondary and borderland discourse; for others, the transitions are more difficult, or the boundaries are flagrantly transgressed in an attempt to contest the discursive space of the school.

From an emancipatory standpoint, one might argue that learning mentors are radical agents of change, aiming to franchise the disenfranchised. The case could be made for learning mentors to practice a 'border pedagogy'. Aronowitz and Giroux (1991) define border pedagogy as a practice that calls into question forms of subordination that create inequities among different groups as they live out their lives. From this position, learning mentors deliberately identify with and advocate for the disenfranchised young people and their families, with whom they work.

However, learning mentors' work is often more complex than the emancipatory standpoint can account for. Learning mentors do aim to enfranchise the disenfranchised, but they are also employees in schools. So they are subject to the often competing demands of school leaders, standards and policy outcomes. An emancipatory standpoint cannot account for the complex and often highly skilled ways they negotiate these demands and power relationships. Learning mentors do not just have 'solidary' responsibility to the young people with whom they work and their families. As employees, they also have responsibilities to school leaders and have to meet the outcome-driven demands of policy. This is particularly urgent as the funding streams change from grant-funded programmes to mainstreamed provision.

The possibilities of a post-structuralist position

The post-structuralist position draws on emancipatory theories and critiques of schooling, without assuming that practitioners have only a 'solidary' responsibility to young people and their families. From a post-structuralist standpoint, learning mentors look for opportunities to open up institutional spaces. They understand that power relationships inhere in practice and therefore look at setting up conditions for respectful dialogue with young people and their families.

Learning mentor practice in schools varies considerably. Some of it could be labelled as neo-liberal, some emancipatory and some post-structuralist. Practice largely depends on the leadership and culture of the school, the values and convictions of the learning mentor and the way in which policy is interpreted locally. In identifying and selecting case studies to be included in this book, I have made judgements about what I consider to be good practice.

You will see in these pages an emphasis on how learning mentors contribute to making schools better places for pupils. They help them to achieve and engage rather than merely comply with the more narrowly defined goals of attainment and attendance. I suggest that this is not crass neo-liberal support for the standards agenda. I argue in chapter three, citing Fullan's (2003) work, that the 'moral imperative' of school leadership is for forms of schooling that are responsive to a class-based analysis of the achievement and engagement gaps. And I return again and again to learning! The learning I mean is a broader journey of personal, social, emotional and intellectual growth, facilitated in and through a 'working alliance'. So it is useful to explore the discourses of learning in a little more detail.

Learning discourses

This book is positioned within particular discourses of learning. In his paper 'Against Learning' Grey explores and refutes the dominant 'learning discourse' which, he argues, is relentlessly performative. Learning is – and should be – a highly contested term and it is important to explore how this book is positioned within discursive constructions of what counts as learning. I look briefly at three different learning discourses, which I will call the transmission model, the instrumentalist model and the transitive model.

The transmission model of learning

The transmission model of learning is essentially politically conservative and perhaps best exemplified by Mr Gradgrind's definition of learning in Dickens' novel *Hard Times* as 'facts, facts, facts'. In this model, learning is the reception of factual knowledge and information, which is differentiated in order to double as a means of social control that reproduces socio-economic stratification by preparing children and young people for different positions in the labour market. This is the familiar 'empty vessel' idea where children and young people are viewed as empty receptors into which adults pour factual knowledge and information. This largely Victorian notion of learning is now considered to be outdated, but unfortunately survives in insidious ways, like the way that space is organised in some classrooms. From within this model, learning is controlled by the adult and completely regulative.

The instrumentalist model of learning

This is the currently dominant neo-liberal model of learning to which Grey (2001) takes such exception. It is driven largely by pressure on schools to get children and young people to 'attain' against a particular set of narrowly prescribed outcomes or learning objectives. However, if we are to take a position *against* something as Grey does, we have to establish something in its place. And this brings us to the learning discourse that I explore and espouse in this book: the transitive model.

The transitive model of learning

Constructions of learning can be drawn from within emancipatory theory. Boal writes:

> Freire talks about the transitivity of true teaching: the teacher is not a person who unloads knowledge ... the teacher is a person who has a particular area of knowledge, transmits it to the pupil and at the same time, receives another knowledge in return, since the pupil also has his or her own area of knowledge. The least a teacher has to learn from a pupil is how the pupil learns. Pupils are different from one another; they learn differently. Teaching is transitivity. Democracy. Dialogue. (Boal, 1998:19)

In the transmission model and arguably also the instrumentalist model, learning is governed by an intransitive relationship in which knowledge is transmitted from the adult to the child and there is a focus on outcomes – on the child's demonstrated knowledge, measured as attainment.

In a transitive model, learning is an active, mediated, dialogic social process in which participants learn from each other. Adults as mediators or facilitators are the means by which the child or young person acts upon and is acted upon by the social (Daniels, 2001). I will return to this definition of learning as social practice and explore the links to John Dewey's theories of democratic learning, Vygotsky's social development theories and Lave and Wenger's situated learning theory in chapter six of this book. However, I want to return briefly to Fielding's taxonomy. I proposed above that the most useful standpoint (or the one that offers us most possibilities for developing a model of learning mentor practice) is the post-structuralist position. The post-structuralist position draws on emancipatory theory, but is critical of its totalising narratives. Lave and Wenger's situated learning theory provides a useful way of understanding the social and transitive nature of learning that includes the conditional and the contingent. Lave and Wenger propose:

> A person's intentions to learn are engaged and the meaning of learning is configured through the process of becoming a full participant in a socio-cultural practice. This social process includes, indeed it subsumes, the learning of knowledgeable skills. (Lave and Wenger, 1991: 29)

Becoming a full participant in a socio-cultural practice is what Lave and Wenger define as a process of 'legitimate peripheral participation'. They maintain that there is 'no illegitimate peripheral participant':

> The form that legitimacy of participation takes is a defining characteristic of ways of belonging, and is therefore not only a crucial condition for learning, but a constitutive element of its content. (Lave and Wenger, 1991: 35)

I return to the idea of belonging as a crucial condition for learning and consider how learning mentors create the social conditions for belonging. First let us look, from a post-structuralist standpoint, at the notion of peripherality:

> Peripherality suggests that there are multiple, varied, more- or less-engaged and inclusive ways of being located in the fields of participation defined by a community... legitimate peripherality is a complex notion, implicated in social structures involving relations of power. As a place in which one moves towards more-intensive participation, peripherality is an empowering position. As a place in which one is kept from participating more fully ... it is a disempowering position. (Lave and Wenger, 1991: 35-36)

Learning mentors actively seek sites of legitimate peripheral participation in schools within which children can be engaged as learners, but these sites are often shifting, conditional and contingent. In schools that seek more equitable, democratic and inclusive forms of organisation, legitimate peripheral participation will be an empowering position and learning mentor practice will be most effective.

Working and writing in a paradox

'Without contraries is no progression.' William Blake
(*The Marriage of Heaven and Hell*)

The learning discourses are more complex than this cursory analysis allows for. We cannot simply reject the instrumentalist model and measures of learning *because it carries socio-economic power.* Further, it would be politically naïve and exceedingly foolish to ignore the demands of policy and current school inspection regime. So I make no apology for positioning learning mentors in the policy context (in chapter two), and demonstrating how learning mentors contribute to raising standards and hence, to school improvement (in chapters three and four).

The importance of a post-structuralist position is that it enables me to write dialectically within a paradox: to evidence how learning mentors contribute to the *doxa* (or dominant policy position) in which the functional drive for standards marginalises the personal, and also to demonstrate how learning mentors' work operates within an antithetical person-centred position in which 'the functional is used for the sake of the personal' (Fielding, 2004: 211). It is in and through this contradiction, this dialectic, this equivocal space, that I hope to open up sites of struggle and argue that learning mentors' work creates one possibility for achieving more equitable forms of schooling.

There *is* a moral responsibility (Fullan, 2003) to close the achievement and engagement gap and learning mentors must, and do, contribute to this. In demonstrating how learning mentors help to close the achievement and engagement gap (in chapter three) and contribute to school improvement (in chapter four), I am not suggesting that they should be constituted in, or constrained by, the standards agenda. On the contrary, their work exposes the narrow and instrumentalist forms of learning that serve to create and sustain the achievement and engagement gap. By working within a transitive and social model of learning that actually supports achievement and engagement, learning mentors' work opens up 'learning' as a site of struggle.

Learning mentors help to make the rules of participation in the learning discourse(s) explicit, and broker access to learning through participation. In this sense, learning mentors are *learning discourse guides*:

> Mercer draws on Lave and Wenger's work and the situated learning concepts of 'legitimate peripheral participation' and 'guided participation' in his proposal that we could seek to understand how more experienced members of communities act as 'discourse guides' as children are supported in their appropriation of collective thinking. (Daniels, 2001: 123)

What makes learning mentors different from other mentoring provision is the focus on learning. This is why I try to outline what I mean by learning, in relation to learning mentors' work, and to offer a position within learning discourses. I return to this idea and look at a functional definition of learning mentoring in chapter five, exploring theories that underpin professional practice in groups with close competence links (in chapter six) and work towards a theory-based model of learning mentoring (in chapter seven).

The third and final section of this book is the most important. Here, I begin mapping learning mentor practice against an existing set of functions, using case studies from the community of practice. The 35 case studies have enormous value in terms of generating knowledge and understanding of the range of learning mentor practices in schools. In arguing the value of case study research, Colley cites Bourdieu and Wacquant (1992: 77): 'You must immerse yourself in the particular to find in it the invariant... A particular case that is well-constructed ceases to be particular' (cited in Colley, 2003: 3). Colley goes on to propose that case studies provide 'rich data with multiple dimensions, reflecting a variety of perspectives... at an experiential level that is usually hidden from view' (2003: 4).

For the past two and a half years, I have immersed myself in the field of learning mentor practice, in a co-ordinating and programme management role. I have never ceased to be amazed by the many ways in which learning mentors help to make schools better places, and I hope this book brings them into view.

This book is overtly striving to influence policy makers and school leaders on the benefits of learning mentor practice. I hope it offers insights into the policy context and learning mentor practice but I am aware that these insights will be counter-pointed with moments of blindness. There will be moments when I may slip back into the very discourses of instrumentalist learning and neo-liberal reasoning that I seek to resist. As any good post-structuralist knows, subjectivity is plural and complex. We move in and out of discursive positions and it is difficult to maintain a coherent position within one preferred subject position. I do not apologise for these slippages and moments of blindness. I quoted Blake at the start: there are undoubtedly contradictions or perhaps multiple dimensions in the material presented here. I hope that out of these contradictions comes progress, and that this book will initiate a constructive dialogue about learning mentor practice. As Egan says, ideas 'serve as a starting point for your reflection... Don't just swallow them. Analyse, reflect on, and debate them' (2002: 46).

PART ONE
POLICY AND SCHOOL
IMPROVEMENT

2

Learning mentors in the policy context

L earning mentors are in a fledgling profession in a rapidly changing policy context in which they are vulnerable to the vagaries of change. At the same time as being lauded as the most successful strand of the initiative that gave birth to them, they are subject to the competing demands of an increasingly complex policy field. This chapter provides an overview of the national policy background, discusses the policy complexities affecting school leaders and learning mentors at this historic moment in English education and tries to locate learning mentors within an international policy context. It makes the case that learning mentors are essential to schools' capacity to deliver on policy developments.

The policy background: Excellence in Cities

In 1999, the Labour Government in England launched Excellence in Cities, its flagship initiative for raising attainment in inner cities. The four core aims of the Excellence in Cities programmes, as they were articulated in 1999, are:

- to have high expectations of every individual

- to increase the diversity of provision

■ for schools to work together collaboratively in networks

■ to extend opportunity and enhance equality. (DfEE, 1999a)

Originally, the Excellence in Cities initiative focused on secondary schools in six large urban conurbations: inner London, Birmingham, Manchester and Salford, Liverpool and Knowsley, Leeds and Bradford and Sheffield and Rotherham. The rationale for this was a perceived 'urgency' to support inner city education, 'recognising its special characteristics and providing greater challenge and support' (DfEE, 1999a: 2).

In 2000, after a favourable evaluation of the first year, the government decided to fund an 'extension pilot' in the primary sector. Since then, the Excellence in Cities initiative has grown exponentially and now covers fifty-seven local education authorities in England and many more 'Excellence Clusters'. Excellence Clusters are smaller, geographically defined areas of deprivation outside the large urban conurbations. According to the DfES, there are approximately one thousand secondary schools and over a thousand primary schools involved in the initiative (DfES, 2004b).

The learning mentor programme is one of a number of Excellence in Cities programmes, aiming primarily to support schools in raising achievement and improving participation by improving attendance and reducing exclusions.

A functional definition of learning mentors is 'to provide support and guidance to children, young people and those engaged with them, by removing barriers to learning in order to promote effective participation, enhance individual learning, raise aspirations and achieve full potential' (Sauvé Bell Associates, 2003). I will return to this definition, exploring it in chapter five, and then analyse detailed learning mentor functions in greater depth, in section three.

The learning mentor programme is widely perceived to be the most successful of the Excellence in Cities programmes. In

2003, the schools' inspectorate, Ofsted, produced a report on Excellence in Cities and Education Action Zones, another of the government's initiatives to encourage partnerships between schools, their communities, local businesses in defined geographic areas to find innovative solutions to educational issues, which stated:

> The most successful and popular of the EIC strands is learning mentors. The creation of these posts has been greatly welcomed and has enabled the majority of schools to enhance the quality of support they offer to disaffected, underachieving or vulnerable pupils. (Ofsted, 2003a)

Policy developments: 'Re-engineering' Excellence in Cities, *Every Child Matters* and The Children Act (2004)

The Excellence in Cities initiative is widely perceived to have succeeded in its aim of raising attainment in the inner cities and in area of deprivation outside of cities. According to figures published on the DfES website, 'the average rate of improvement across whole authority [Excellence in Cities] partnerships, in Excellence Clusters, in EIC Action Zones and in EAZs was faster than schools outside the programme' (DfES, 2004c). In the GCSE results in 2003, 'schools in Excellence in Cities whole authority partnerships improved at more than twice the rate of schools elsewhere with average gains of 2.5 percentage points compared to 1.2 percentage points in non-EIC schools' (DfES, 2004c).

The Excellence in Cities initiative was originally funded to 2004. In the face of the perceived success of the initiative, the government announced that it would extend funding to 2006, significantly expanding the initiative in this two-year period.

However, at the same time, the government is aware of the need to sustain these improvements beyond 2006 and continue to target resources effectively in the inner cities and areas of deprivation. Consequently the DfES has embarked on 're-engineering' Excellence in Cities, a policy development aiming to reshape Excellence in Cities to:

- increase the impact of EIC resources and activities on teaching and learning

- help effective partnerships concentrate on outcomes rather than fragmented strands...

- encourage the integration of other DfES targeted programmes within EIC activities so as to make the best use of all school improvement funding and support that each school gets...

- provide better challenge and support for EIC partnerships, particularly those who have not seen great overall improvements in pupil attainment. (DfES, 2004c)

In order to achieve this, the government proposes to rationalise funding streams, collapsing many of the grant-funded initiatives like Excellence in Cities into a single standards grant. Effectively, this means that school leaders will be able to make decisions about how best to target resources to meet school improvement priorities. But, as I argue in chapter three, school improvement is a bigger agenda than simply raising standards. Fullan (2003) argues that school leaders have a moral imperative to close the gap between the highest achieving and lowest achieving pupils. This moral imperative also extends to providing inclusive learning opportunities, engaging the community of learners and creating a sense of belonging. In this more broadly defined school improvement agenda, learning mentors have an essential role.

The re-engineering of Excellence in Cities is one of many policy developments potentially affecting learning mentors employed in schools. Other significant developments are the *Every Child Matters* agenda and school workforce reform.

In 2003, following the enquiry into the high profile child-death case of Victoria Climbié, the government published a Green Paper: *Every Child Matters* (DfES, 2003b). This set the agenda for fundamental structural reform of services, reform of service delivery and workforce reform.

The rationale for this large-scale reform agenda is both to 'protect children and maximise their potential' (DfES, 2003b: 5). The aim is to ensure that every child has the chance to fulfil their potential. This aim is scaffolded on five outcomes, which the government proposes mattered most to children and young people, following consultation with them:

- being healthy: enjoying good physical and mental health and living a healthy lifestyle

- staying safe: being protected from harm and neglect

- enjoying and achieving: getting the most out of life and developing the skills for adulthood

- making a positive contribution: being involved with the community and society and not engaging in antisocial or offending behaviour

- economic well-being: not being prevented by economic disadvantage from achieving their full potential in life. (DfES, 2003b: 6-7)

These outcomes are central to the programme of change outlined in *Every Child Matters: Change for Children* (DfES, 2004e) and are at the heart of the reforms set out in the Children Act (2004). It will become clear that learning mentors are well placed to help deliver these outcomes, particularly supporting children and young people to 'enjoy and achieve' and 'make a positive contribution'.

It is not within the scope of this book to outline the detail of the reform agenda, except in so far as it impacts on learning mentors. The Green Paper sets out a commitment to increasing the number of learning mentors, in the broader policy context of inter-agency working, a closer integration of services and workforce reform. *Every Child Matters: Change for Children* (DfES, 2004e) sets out a national framework for every local authority in the country to produce a children and young people's plan, that will shift children's services from intervention to prevention. This transformation of the children's workforce is underway. The DfES has set up a Children's Workforce Unit to lead on workforce reform. One of the main functions of this unit is to look at occupational competence across the range of professionals working with children and explore how to develop skills and teamwork across services.

At the same time, the School Workforce Unit in the DfES is leading policy on 'remodelling' the school workforce. As learning mentors are employed in schools, it is worth considering why they are located, in the policy context, in the Children's Workforce as opposed to the School's Workforce. The answer to this is complex, and part of the changing vision for schools in England. *Every Child Matters* puts the case for the co-location of services and a much greater emphasis on multi-agency work. The Labour Government has launched a variety of multi-agency pilots, including the 'Behaviour Improvement Project' with multi-agency Behaviour, Education and Support Teams working to support a small number of schools in a geographically defined area, and 'Extended Schools' which provide a greater number of multi-agency services on site. In this context, the schools workforce can be defined as those professionals (teachers and support staff) who are responsible for teaching and learning in the context of the curriculum. The children's workforce can be defined as those professionals (including learning mentors, education welfare officers, personal advisors, health, social services and other professionals) working in a multi-agency context to improve children's life chances, including their engagement with and participation in learning.

Learning mentors are therefore at the front line of change and will be essential if schools are to deliver the five outcomes in the new Ofsted framework for inspecting schools which comes into effect on 1 September 2005, and the fundamental reforms set out in *Every Child Matters* and the *Children Act* (2004), including common assessment, information sharing, earlier intervention and better preventative work, integration and multi-agency working, and work with families.

At the same time as *Every Child Matters* was being formulated, the DfES commissioned a national exercise to develop *National Occupational Standards* across three professional groups: learning mentors, education welfare officers and Connexions personal advisors. The Green Paper refers to the need for occupational mapping and the identification of professional competence links across all professionals working with children.

The National Occupational Standards for Learning Development and Support Services for children, young people and those who care for them were signed off by ministers in December 2003. They form a comprehensive set of standards or units, identifying areas of professional competence. They are an important step in recognising that learning mentoring is skilled work.

Department for Education and Skills' five year strategy and the personalised learning agenda

In 2004, the government launched its *Five Year Strategy for Children and Learners* (DfES, 2004f). A key part of this strategy is 'personalised learning'. Personalised learning appears to be a concept that is, as yet, uncertain in the policy context. David Milliband, then Minister of State for School Standards, defines it as an offer.

> A personalised offer in education depends on really knowing the strengths and weaknesses of individual students. So the biggest driver for change is assessment for learning and the use of data and dialogue to diagnose every student's learning needs. (Milliband, 2004: 4)

He goes on to define five key elements of the personalised offer: assessment for learning, teaching and learning strategies built on individual needs, curriculum choice, a 'radical' approach to school organisation to which workforce reform is key and an inter-agency approach to supporting schools. In his *Choice and Voice in Personalised Learning* speech, Milliband then describes voice as the 'active demand side... in choices about schools, voices and activities' (Milliband, 2004: 7-8).The rhetoric of

Milliband's speech does little to allay concerns that New Labour's policies are based on a rampant 'individualism' in which choice and voice continue to be the domain of the privileged few, in contrast to approaches that stress the renewal of civic society and community.

Charles Leadbeater, Senior Research Associate with DEMOS, a British educational think-tank, puts forward a more progressive understanding of personalised learning in a pamphlet entitled *Learning about personalistion.* Leadbeater questions how the education script can be re-written so that it is more responsive to users. He puts forward an argument for the users of education to have a voice in what services look like – to rewrite the 'script' of services. He calls this 'personalisation through participation' (Leadbeater, 2004: 14).

Leadbeater defines the characteristics that a personalised public service (in this case, school) would have. The first of these is identified as *intimate consultation*: 'professionals working with users to help unlock their needs, preferences and aspirations, through an extended dialogue' (Leadbeater, 2004: 14). Learning mentors are uniquely placed in schools to conduct this extended dialogue and to help unlock the potential of children and young people.

Michael Fielding, at the Centre for Educational Innovation at the University of Sussex, argues that Leadbeater's approach is to beat a middle way between the 'rather overdone and too often superficial appeal to work with student learning styles, [and] also the potentially much more radical students-as-researchers initiative also championed by the NCSL' (Fielding, 2004:199).

Learning mentors are well placed to deliver on both the more neo-liberal and more emancipatory aspects of the personalised learning agenda, particularly Leadbeater's definition of 'intimate consultation'.

Learning mentors in an international policy context

Helen Colley (2003) documents the 'rise and rise' of mentoring in North America, the United Kingdom and other countries in her critically acclaimed book: *Mentoring for Social Inclusion: a critical approach to nurturing mentoring relationships.*

Colley cites Skinner and Fleming's (1999) analysis of three broad models of youth mentoring in Britain:

- Industrial mentoring in which Education Business Partnerships recruit mentors from local businesses, who are matched to young people with the aim of raising self-esteem and encouraging higher attainment, and ultimately entering the workforce

- 'Positive action' or 'community mentoring' aimed at supporting young people from oppressed groups

- Volunteer mentoring targeting groups of young people 'at risk' and aiming to re-engage young people with formal education, training and employment systems in preparation for entry into the labour market, which Colley calls 'engagement mentoring'. (Colley, 2003: 16-18)

Arguably, learning mentors fall into a fourth category, which Skinner and Fleming's analysis could not have included since Excellence in Cities was being launched in the same year as their paper was published. While Colley makes passing reference to Excellence in Cities and learning mentors as the 'culmination' of a trend that has moved mentoring to centre-stage in England (Colley, 2003: 12), her specific analysis of mentoring remains firmly located in Skinner and Fleming's third category. Her critical analysis of mentoring nevertheless resonates in important ways, and I engage with some of her ideas in the chapters that follow.

It is less the case that learning mentors fall into a fourth category of 'mentoring' – since, as we have seen, the focus on learning makes learning mentoring different from other mentoring programmes – it is more useful to demonstrate professional competence links with other professional groups, both nationally and internationally. In England, the recent functional mapping and *National Occupational Standards* has evidenced professional competence links with education welfare officers and Connexions personal advisors. Internationally, learning mentoring has close professional competence links with social pedagogy (predominantly in Europe) and child and youth care work (predominantly in the United States and Canada).

Social pedagogy is a little-known concept in the United Kingdom. Smith argues that the tradition of social pedagogy has become associated with social work, but that this obscures its educational imperative (Smith, 1999: 1). Smith explores the contribution of Friedrich Schleiermacher, a nineteenth century German philosopher who argued for 'education for community'. Smith proposes that this 'linking of pedagogy with community and democracy has remained a key theme – and can be seen in the work of later writers such as Dewey and Freire' (Smith, 1999: 2-3). We return to these theorists in chapter six.

According to Walter Lorenz, social pedagogy includes a concept of promoting well-being of the whole person (Lorenz 1994, cited in Vitler 2002: 1). This includes an educational function.

Smith cites Cannan's definition of social pedagogy as:

> A perspective, including social action which aims to promote human welfare through child rearing and education practices; and to prevent or ease social problems by providing people with the means to manage their own lives, and make changes in their circumstances. (Cannan *et al.*, 1992: 73-74, cited in Smith, 1999: 5)

So how is social pedagogy different from social work and youth work?

Smith proposes that pedagogy and casework 'appeal to different traditions... the taking of the notion of 'pedagogy' (or education) into the way you name yourself makes a direct appeal to a particular body of theory and practice. The title social work (like youth work) connects with a certain array of institutions and agencies' (Smith, 1999: 7).

Daniels argues for the implicit definition of the 'social' implied in the word pedagogy itself:

> My suggestion is that the term pedagogy should be construed as referring to forms of social practice which shape and form the cognitive, affective and moral development of individuals. If pedagogic practices are understood as those which influence the formation of identity as well as learning outcomes as defined in, say, test scores, then a form of social theory is required that will allow us to model and investigate the factors which may be exercising some effect. (Daniels: 2001: 1)

Daniels also points out that there is not a strong tradition of teaching and learning as 'pedagogic practice' in England. One contribution I hope this book will make is to bring learning as social practice into view. I return to this idea in chapter six, exploring social pedagogical theories, particularly Vygotsky's contribution.

Arguably, social pedagogy has closer links in England with the tradition of informal or community education than with social work or youth work. Vitler argues that recent government initiatives 'such as the Connexions Service, which provides careers advice and support to young people, are more akin to social pedagogy in its approach than were previous ways of working with young people (Vitler 2002: 1). Equally, learning mentoring has strong competence links with social pedagogy in its focus on an education function, social activity and a holistic approach to children and young people that promotes well-being. Social pedagogues and learning mentors both provide 'positive role models as educated professionals for children, particularly for children who have not seen education as offering them anything' (Vitler 2002: 2).

mentoring creates a possibility of making schools ... es for more children, then another important link to soc.. ..dagogy emerges. Cannan and Warren have begun the task of exploring theory and practice of practitioners working with children and families to 'find ways of working together to promote environments in which children can flourish and ... develop forms of public life that are friendly to children, young people and their parents' (1997: 1). They argue that it is necessary to recast children and family services in a community development framework, which they call 'social action' (1997: 1). I offer this connection to 'social action' in the hope that it will be picked up by the practice community and explored further as children's services are developed by local authorities.

Demonstrating competence links with a long-standing professional group is important because it enables the exploration of theories that underpin and inform social pedagogic practice. Learning mentoring, as a new and emerging professional group, has not yet developed coherent links to theoretical perspectives. It is however not only the European tradition of social pedagogy that offers a professional group with close competence links. It is also important to consider Child and Youth Care Work in North America.

The American Association for Child and Youth Care Practice (ACYCP) describes the field as focusing on:

> Infants, children and adolescents... within the context of the family, the community and the life span. The developmental-ecological perspective emphasises the interaction between persons and their physical and social environments, including cultural and political settings. (ACYCP, 2002: 4)

The North American Certification Project (NACP) identifies five domains: professionalism, applied human development, relationship and communication, development practice methods and cultural and human diversity (ACYCP, 2002). Each of these domains is further broken down into elements of professional competence.

In the United Kingdom, *The National Occupational Standards for Learning, Development and Support Services* were developed by three training organisations (ENTO, PAULO and TOPSS, 2003a) for the DfES. The standards consist of sixty-one 'Units of Competence,' which relate directly to individual job functions. Qualifications are being developed, based on the *National Occupational Standards*. The national vocational qualification identifies seven of the sixty-one units of competence as being mandatory for learning mentors pursuing a level three qualification. Five of these units are common across the three professional groups: learning mentors, education welfare officers and Connexions personal advisors:

- Contribute to the protection of children and young people from abuse

- Ensure their own actions reduce risks to health and safety

- Review their contribution to the service

- Enable children and young people to find out about and use services and facilities

- Operate within networks

Two units of competence relate specifically to learning mentor job functions:

- Facilitate children and young people's learning and development through mentoring

- Support the child or young person's successful transfer and transition in learning and development contexts

In order to complete the National Vocational Qualification at level 3, learning mentors must evidence their competence and underlying knowledge and understanding against the seven units of competence described above, and a further two units chosen from an optional list of twenty-one units.

Table 1 sets out the professional competence links between learning mentors and child and youth care workers. The table shows the correlation between the seven units of competence defined within the national vocational qualifications framework as being mandatory for learning mentors, and the Association of Child and Youth Care Practice (ACYCP) competencies for professional child and youth work practitioners from the North American Certification Project. In establishing competence links, I am not suggesting that child and youth work practitioners perform exactly the same job functions as learning mentors, but rather that there is enough evidence of competence links to learn from the United States and Canadian professions.

Interestingly, there is also a strong correlation in the policy context between the United Kingdom and British Columbia. It was a high-profile child-death case in British Columbia that resulted in wide-scale policy developments and radical restructuring in the mid-nineties. After a child death inquiry, the government decided to form a single Ministry for Children and Families with the aim of amalgamating services. In the United Kingdom, the Children Act (2004), the legislative response to the Green Paper, *Every Child Matters*, establishes a Children's Commissioner for England 'to represent the views and interests of children and report to Parliament on progress against the outcomes for children and young people (DfES, 2004d: 14). A new Minister for Children, Young People and Families has been created and the integration of national policy for children and young people now sits within the DfES. The Children Act (2004) also requires local authorities to produce a children and young people's plan which will provide the strategic framework for local restructuring, integrated commissioning of services and integrated service delivery.

Learning mentors are therefore part of a changing children's workforce. This is the time for us to examine international examples and learn more about policy implementation and

Table 1: Professional competence links between learning mentors and child and youth care workers

UK National Occupational Standards (NOS) for Learning, Development and Support Services for children and young people and those who care for them	ACYCP competencies for professional child and youth work practitioners (from North American Certification Project)	Description of the match between elements of competence defined in the NOS and ACYCP
Standard/unit of competence Facilitate children and young people's learning and development through mentoring **Elements of competence** *Learning mentors must be able to:* Identify the learning and development needs of children and young people Plan with children and young people how learning and development needs will be addressed through mentoring Mentor children and young people to achieve identified outcomes		Child and youth care workers use developmental-ecological assessment to assess development in different domains and across different contexts and assess the individual needs of children and young people and their families (applied human development domain). Child and youth care workers are expected to encourage children and young people to participate in assessment and goal setting in intervention planning and the development of individual educational and developmental plans (intervention planning, programme planning and activity planning competence in the domain of developmental practice methods). Practice methods are drawn from developmental-ecological perspective and include many functions that are common to learning mentoring: • supporting development • designing and implementing programmes... which integrate developmental, preventative and therapeutic objectives into the life-space

Table 1: Professional competence links between learning mentors and child and youth care workers (continued)

| Standard/unit of competence | Elements of competence
Learning mentors must be able to: | UK National Occupational Standards (NOS) for Learning, Development and Support Services for children and young people and those who care for them
ACYCP competencies for professional child and youth work practitioners (from North American Certification Project) | Description of the match between elements of competence defined in the NOS and ACYCP |
|---|---|---|---|
| | | | • individualising developmental, preventative and therapeutic plans to reflect differences in culture/ human diversity, background, temperament, personality and differential rates of development |
| | | | • designing and implementing group work, counselling and behavioural guidance |
| | | | • employing developmentally sensitive expectations in setting appropriate boundaries and limits |
| | | | • creating and maintaining a safe and growth-promoting environment |
| | | | • making risk management decisions that reflect sensitivity for individuality, age, development, culture and human diversity while also ensuring a safe and growth-promoting environment. |
| | Review the effectiveness of mentoring with children and young people | | Child and youth care workers are expected to work with children and young people to assess and monitor progress and to revise plans as needed (Intervention planning competence in the domain of developmental practice methods) |

Table 1: Professional competence links between learning mentors and child and youth care workers (continued)

UK National Occupational Standards (NOS) for Learning, Development and Support Services for children and young people and those who care for them		ACYCP competencies for professional child and youth work practitioners (from North American Certification Project)
Standard/unit of competence	**Elements of competence** *Learning mentors must be able to:*	**Description of the match between elements of competence defined in the NOS and ACYCP**
Support the child or young person's successful transfer and transition in learning and development contexts	1. Plan for transfer and transition 2. Support the child or young person to prepare for transfer or transition 3. Monitor the success of transfer and transition and identify continued support needs	No match.
Contribute to the protection of children and young people from abuse	1. Identify signs and symptoms of possible abuse 2. Respond to a child's disclosure of abuse 3. Inform other professionals about suspected abuse 4. Promote children's awareness of personal safety and abuse	Child and youth care workers are expected to have awareness of Law and Regulations (professionalism domain). Specifically, they must know the legal responsibility for reporting child abuse and neglect and the consequences of failure to report.
Ensure your own actions reduce risks to health and safety	1. Identify the hazards and evaluate the risks in your workplace 2. Reduce the risks to health and safety in your workplace	Child and youth care workers must have health and safety competence (under the domain of developmental practice methods). Specifically, they must incorporate environmental safety into the arrangement of space, storage of equipment and supplies and the design and implementation of activities, and the current health, hygiene and nutrition practices.

Table 1: Professional competence links between learning mentors and child and youth care workers (continued)

UK National Occupational Standards (NOS) for Learning, Development and Support Services for children and young people and those who care for them		ACYCP competencies for professional child and youth work practitioners (from North American Certification Project)	Description of the match between elements of competence defined in the NOS and ACYCP
Standard/unit of competence	**Elements of competence** *Learning mentors must be able to:*		
Review own contribution to the service	1. Assess own contribution to the work of the service 2. Develop oneself to achieved work requirements		Child and youth care workers are expected to reflect on their practice and performance by evaluating their own performance, identify needs for professional growth and give and receive constructive feedback. (Professional development and behaviour competence in the domain of professionalism.)
Enable children and young people to find out about and use services and facilities	1. Enable children and young people to find out about services and facilities 2. Enable children and young people to use services and facilities		Child and youth care workers must locate and critically evaluate community resources for programmes and activities and connect children, youth and families to them (in the domain of developmental practice methods).
Operate within networks	1. Maintain membership of networks 2. Exchange information within networks		There is no specific expectation for child and youth care workers to operate within networks, however, the professionalism domain sets out the expectation to have an awareness of the profession, to access local and national professional activities and to contribute to the ongoing development of the field.

professional practice. Additionally, the examination of the theories informing child and young care practice – particularly the psychoeducational model – provides an important starting point in developing a model of learning mentor practice. The psychoeducational model is explored in chapter six.

This chapter has provided an overview of the national policy background, and attempted to locate learning mentors within an international policy context. I have argued that learning mentors are essential to schools' capacity to deliver on national policy developments. The current policy context, with its focus on building services around the needs of children and families rather than the needs of individual services, creates a climate of possibility. Within this climate, innovative school leaders will seize the opportunity for structural change in order to create educational institutions that will meet the needs of more (or all!) children and young people. It is this argument that is developed in the next chapter.

3

Redefining school improvement – the challenge to school leaders

Moral purpose of the highest order is having a system where all students learn, the gap between high and low performance becomes greatly reduced, and what people learn enables them to be successful citizens and workers in a morally based knowledge society. (Fullan, 2003: 29)

School improvement is a far bigger agenda than raising standards. Fullan (2003) argues that school leaders have a moral imperative to close the gap between the highest achieving and lowest achieving pupils. I maintain that learning mentors are an important part of a school's resources for addressing inequality related to the achievement gap. That schools should provide inclusive learning opportunities, engaging the community of learners and creating a sense of belonging is now an important part of school self-evaluation and a focus in the new Ofsted framework. In this more broadly defined school improvement agenda, learning mentors have an essential role. Following Fullan, I suggest that school leaders' moral responsibilities do not end with school improvement: school leaders must seize the opportunities created by policy to effect structural and system changes that promote equality.

The gap between high and low pupil performance – a product of inequality

The Programme for International Student Assessment (PISA), part of the Organisation for Economic Co-operation and Development (OECD), is an attempt to measure pupil achievement across OECD member countries, and some which are not members. By assessing fifteen-year old pupils, PISA provides an indication of the overall performance of school systems. PISA conducted its first assessments in 2000. It intends to continue to survey the knowledge and skills of fifteen-year olds in the principle industrialised countries every three years. Unfortunately, the government has not produced sufficient data for England to participate in the 2003 survey.

Alongside an assessment of knowledge and skills, PISA also gathers contextual information from pupils about themselves and from school leaders about their schools. Significantly, the PISA report *Knowledge for Skills and Life* (2001) analyses the impact of family background on attainment.

The association between background and pupil performance in the UK is strong: there is a mean difference of 97 score points – approximately one proficiency level – between the least advantaged pupils and the most advantaged, as based on their parents' occupations. In the PISA report, the association between family background and pupil performance differs greatly from one country to another, with Korea at one extreme (with a relatively small difference of 33 score points) and the United Kingdom at the other, with only five countries with larger point score differences below it. There is clearly a moral case to narrow this gap between high and low pupil performances. The Excellence in Cities initiative is one positive attempt that the government has made to narrow this gap.

There is not only a case to be made in terms of family background and class. There is much data and research evidence that other groups of pupils are more likely to find themselves in lower attaining groups. Ofsted (1999) found that 'at secondary level, the data indicate that Black Caribbean students are in some cases the lowest achieving group at GCSE level.' In 2000, Ofsted issued an alarming press release stating: 'African-Caribbean and Pakistani pupils have drawn least benefit from the rising levels of attainment: the gap between them and their white peers is larger now than a decade ago.'

Gilborn and Mirza (2000) however, warn of the potential negative stereotyping associated with the assumption that all pupils from particular minority ethnic groups 'underachieve'. As they say, 'differences in average achievement between social groups raise cause for concern but do not, in themselves, prove anything about the potential of those groups. The reasons for such relative 'underachievement' are multiple and patterns of inequality are not fixed' (Gilborn and Mirza, 2000: 7). They quote evidence from Ofsted showing that any one group, for example African-Caribbean pupils whose achievement is ranked poorly in national measures, may actually be doing relatively well in some schools. They emphasise that 'difference in attainment between groups can be part of a necessary analysis of inequalities in educational outcomes' (*ibid*).

Similarly, Colley warns of the pitfalls inherent in the government's policy documents that use social exclusion data (like the PISA report identifying the gap between high and low pupil performance as a function of family background) to promote 'the idea that the attitudes, values and beliefs of students and families are themselves a major cause of their (self)exclusion' (2003: 26). Colley argues for the need to alter the policy discourse from social exclusion back to social inequality (2003: 170).

So rather than speaking about 'underachievement' and 'social exclusion', we should theorise about the gap between high and low pupil performance as a product of unequal structures. A more productive way to understand this gap is

> ...to see it as a process that inflicts on disadvantaged young people [and their families], rather than as a characteristic of

young people themselves [or their families]. In this light, it is no longer young people [or their families] who appear as a threat to society: society and its unequal structures constitute a threat to young people [and their families]. (Colley, 2003: 169)

Learning mentors – a school resource to support achievement

Reframing achievement gaps as a product of social inequality and unequal social structures brings us back to Fullan's moral imperative. In school improvement terms, this means analysing data for trends in pupil attainment that point to inequality and then implementing structural change to ensure that all groups are achieving as well as they can. There is nothing new here: the Ofsted *Framework for Inspecting Schools* (2003b, 2005) requires schools to analyse data in this way and show what interventions they are making to raise achievement for these groups (and presumably narrow the achievement gap). The Race Relations (Amendment) Act 2000 places a statutory duty on schools to monitor their policies and practices and their impact on the attainment of individuals and groups of pupils.

Learning mentors have traditionally been part of the school's resources in identifying underachievement and working with pupils and groups of pupils on the skills for learning to raise achievement. Evaluation of Excellence in Cities in terms of pupil outcomes undertaken by the National Foundation for Education Research found that it is possible to identify the positive impact of learning mentors on attainment outcomes for young people (Morris *et al*, 2004a: 14). Interestingly, the data in the report show different outcomes for pupils in low and high performing schools. The report defines a 'low' performing school as one in which fewer than 30 percent of the pupils achieved five or more GCSEs at grade C or above; and a high performing school as one which 65 percent of pupils achieved five or more GCSEs in the year preceding that in which the young people had embarked on their Key Stage 4 course.

For young people in low performing schools... seeing a [learn-ing] mentor was associated with a level of performance above that which might be anticipated from their prior attainment. [Young people]... who had seen a [learning] mentor in a low performing school achieved an additional 0.95 points, on average, and so performed 0.15 GCSE points better than their peers who had not seen a [learning] mentor. They obtained higher best eight scores and their average GCSE points per subject were equivalent to their academic peers. They were also one and a half times more likely to have achieved five or more GCSEs at A* to C grades than young people with similar prior attainment and other characteristics who had not been mentored. These findings suggest that, in lower performing schools, learning mentors may have managed successfully to overcome some (if not all) of the barriers to learning faced by their mentees, and indeed, to raise their performance to levels above those that would have been predicted from their Key Stage 3 outcomes. Similar success were noted in high per-forming schools... In those schools, mentees were three times more likely to have achieved three or more GCSEs at A* than those who had not been mentored. (Morris *et al*, 2004a: 19 – 20)

The data in this report indicate a significant positive association between being mentored and achievement. This suggests that learning mentors are one of the resources that enable schools to narrow the achievement gap between the highest and lowest achieving groups.

The case study on page 40 evidences the work of one learning mentor in one primary school to raise achievement for a parti-cular group of pupils.

Twin drivers of school improvement: achievement and engagement

The drive towards raising standards has created a very narrow school improvement focus on pupil attainment and an instru-mentalist model of learning. Even a radical class and race analysis and a re-framing of the key issue in the standards debate as the imperative to narrow the gap between the highest and lowest achievers still locates the debate firmly in the drive towards raising standards. So is narrowing the achievement gap the only moral imperative for school leaders? Surely the drive for social and educational inclusion is essential to an equalities-

---

Case study 1: closing the achievement gap at Whittingham Community Primary School

In order to closely align LM activity with raising achievement, the Senior Leadership Team at Whittingham Primary School undertook an audit of Year 5 pupils, transferring to Year 6. Pupils were identified as underachieving when comparisons were made between their NFER (non verbal reasoning tests) and their actual QCA test results. Underachievers would be those with average NFER and low QCA or high NFER and low or average QCA results. The aim was to raise their level of achievement so that they would reach their potential. Therefore, if a pupil had a high NFER score they should achieve a high QCA or SAT Test result. If a child had an average NFER score they should achieve either a high or average QCA or SAT test result.

Learning mentoring began with this group in year 5 and continued into year 6. There were twenty-four children. One to one mentoring sessions focused on issues such as anger, frustration, friendships, bullying, low self-esteem and lack of confidence. These were issues with which the children had historically had difficulties. The mentoring sessions looked at how these issues affected their learning.

At the beginning of year 6 all of the children identified were achieving below or well below the national average. Their SATs results showed that 83 percent of the mentees had achieved the national average or above.

One boy who was working below level 3 in year 5 achieved level 5 in Maths and Science and level 4 in English when leaving year 6. The other 17 percent showed no improvement in test results but the impact of mentoring sessions was evident in other ways. Parents, teachers and the children at reviews highlighted significant improvements in behaviour, attitude, academic skills and confidence.

led school improvement agenda. Pupil engagement at school is an educational outcome in its own right, and as important as achievement.

First, we need to establish what is meant by inclusion. Increasingly, the government is requiring schools to have regard for the policies and practices of 'inclusive' education. Inclusion, in official guidance, usually puts forward a narrow policy definition relating particularly to pupils with 'special educational needs'. In 1994, UNESCO issued the *Salamanca Statement and Framework for Action on special needs*, calling on governments to 'adopt as a matter of law or policy the principle of inclusive education, enrolling all children in regular schools, unless there is a compelling reason for doing otherwise'. The government responded with a strategy to improve standards for pupils with special educational needs, set out in *Excellence for All Children – meeting special educational needs* (DfEE, 1997). This policy development culminated in the Special Educational Needs and Disability Discrimination Act (2001), which strengthened the right to mainstream education for children and young people with special educational needs. The statutory guidance, *Inclusive Schooling: Children with special educational needs* (DfES, 2001) sets out the case for disability equality in relation to school admissions. Although passing reference is made to National Curriculum 2000, which requires schools to provide a broad and balanced curriculum for all pupils, the focus of much government policy is on assessment, admissions and resources.

Alongside the policy emphasis on inclusive education for pupils with special educational needs, the government was also developing a policy focus on race equality. In response to the Macpherson inquiry into the death of Stephen Lawrence, the government amended the Race Relations Act and the Commission for Race Equality published a *statutory code of practice on the duty to promote Race Equality* (2001). But, strangely, race equality is not conceptualised as part of the inclusive education agenda.

There is a trend in government thinking not to see the bigger picture of educational inclusion. The government has been better at a broad conceptualisation of social *exclusion* – witness the varied reports from the Social Exclusion Unit – than at broadly conceptualising *inclusion* in education. Recent government initiatives, including Excellence in Cities, Connexions, the Behaviour and Attendance Strategy do not have clearly conceptualised links to educational inclusion.

What is needed is a re-framed, broadly conceptualised definition of inclusion that focuses on equality rather than special educational needs and disability – a definition that will provide a strategic framework for making sense of the codes of practice on special educational needs and race equality as well as a raft of initiatives including Excellence in Cities, Behaviour and Attendance and workforce reform. Inclusion is broadly defined as 'the process of increasing *participation* in their schools and communities of people subjected to exclusionary pressure and practices' (Booth, 1997: 101, my italics). The moral imperative is clear.

Minding another gap: pupil engagement at school

Participation is notoriously difficult to measure. However, PISA has published a thematic report using data on pupil engagement collected during the 2000 survey. Drawing on research in the field, PISA defines the term 'engagement' to refer to 'the extent to which students identify with and value schooling outcomes. Its definition usually comprises a *psychological* component pertaining to students' sense of belonging at school, and a *behavioural* component pertaining to participation in school activities' (Wilms, 2003: 8).

The authors of the PISA report argue that belonging and participation are important educational outcomes in their own right, as they are 'closely tied to students' economic success and long-term health and well-being, and as such deserve to be treated alongside achievement as important [educational] outcomes' (Wilms, 2003:9). Significantly, the five *Every Child*

Matters outcomes informing the new *Framework for Inspecting Schools* (2005) links enjoying and achieving at school – as well as being healthy, staying safe and making a positive contribution to society – with attaining economic well-being.

The PISA survey used two engagement measures: sense of belonging and participation. Sense of belonging 'was based on students' response to six items describing their personal feelings about being accepted by their peers and whether or not they felt lonely, 'like an outsider' or 'out of place" (Wilms, 2003: 18). Participation was measured 'by the frequency of absence, class-skipping and late arrival at school during the two weeks prior to the PISA 2000 survey' (Wilms, 2003: 18). Although the author argues that a broader measure of participation would be desirable, pupil absenteeism was considered to be the most important aspect of participation because trends suggest that there is generally a progression in pupils' withdrawal from school. This narrowly defined concept of participation is open to challenge (see chapter six). Schools pursue a range of activities to involve pupils actively in contributing to their school and in aspects of teaching and learning and school improvement. Some of these are explored in section three.

The results of the PISA 2000 survey on pupil engagement demonstrate that there is a 'high prevalence of students who can be considered disaffected from school in terms of their sense of belonging or their participation. On average, across the OECD countries, about one in four students are classified as having a low sense of belonging, and about one in five students has very low participation' (Wilms, 2003: 25).

The report on pupil engagement also analyses the relationships among achievement and engagement outcomes and their relationship to family background. The evidence from the report shows that there are three dominant risk factors associated with pupil disengagement:

Living in a family of low-socio-economic status – the odds of having a low sense of belonging are about 38 percent greater for students living in low socio-economic status families. Low socio-economic status is also a risk-factor for low participation; the odds ratio is 1:26 (Wilms, 2003: 37-38). In the United Kingdom, the odds of low participation for students in poor families is at least one and a half times as great as the odds for students from average socio-economic families (Wilms, 2003: 40). The report concludes that in virtually every OECD country students from poor families are 'more likely to feel lonely or feel like an outsider in school' (Wilms, 2003: 39) and that living in a high socio-economic status family is a significant protective factor.

Living in a single-parent family – the odds ratio of having a low sense of belonging is 1:17 and low participation is 1:35 (Wilms, 2003).

Being foreign born – the odds ratio of having a low sense of belonging is 1:37 and low participation is 1:30 (Wilms, 2003). The report argues that many students have multiple risk factors.

> For example, many students who have experienced immigration to a new country also live in low socio-economic families. In most countries, a disproportionate number of youths (sic) living in single parent families are also of low socio-economic status. (Wilms, 2003: 48)

While I strongly concur with Wilms that a sense of belonging and participation are educational outcomes in their own right, the relationship between attendance and attainment should not be overlooked. Research by Morris *et al* into pupil attendance data in Excellence in Cities areas, reveals that, using logistical analysis, there is a positive association between attendance and attainment:

> ...as authorised absence decreased, the probability of achieving five A* to C grades increased to just under 65 percent for those with no authorised absence. Conversely, as authorised absence increased, the probability of achieving five A* to C grades decreased... The story with respect to unauthorised

> absence was even more evident, with a rapid decline in the probability of higher levels of achievement amongst those with even two half days more unauthorised absence than the mean of 3.56 half days... Those with high levels of unauthorised absence ... had less than 25 percent probability of achieving five A* to C grades. (Morris *et al*, 2004b: 26-27)

However, Morris *et al* (2004b) argue that a logistical analysis cannot provide the whole picture. Using multi-level modal analysis, they are able to demonstrate that other factors, including prior attainment, individual background characteristics (such as ethnicity, fluency in English and home circumstances) and school factors (including performance levels, type and location) also impact on attendance, and on the relationship between attainment and attendance. Thus it is possible to argue that the strong association between poor attendance and low attainment is also the product of unequal structures and the large gaps in socio-economic status between families in the United Kingdom.

If belonging and participation are educational outcomes in their own right, and if inclusion is about increasing participation in schools and communities of people subjected to exclusionary pressure and practices, then there is clearly also a moral case to narrow this gap between pupils who engage in school and those who feel isolated or who do not participate.

Learning mentors – a school resource to support pupil engagement

Learning mentors are an essential part of schools' capacity to narrow this gap. Morris *et al* in their evaluation report on the impact of Excellence in Cities on pupil outcomes, show that:

> One further emerging impact of the learning mentor strand is worth noting here. There was a clear association between those who had a poor record of attendance in Year 8 or Year 10 respectively and those who had been seen by a [learning] mentor in Year 9 and Year 11 (respectively) suggesting that, in addition to those who are underachieving, learning mentors may also

> be targeting those with a high level of absence... there was evidence that [learning] mentors may have played a role in reducing the level of absence amongst some groups of young people. This was particularly the case among Year 11 pupils who saw themselves as confident and independent learners. (Morris *et al*, 2004a: 19-21)

Significantly, the evaluation report also shows a positive association between working with a learning mentor and a positive change in attitudes to learning and a positive change in attitudes to school:

> More than half of the 430 young people who had been mentored over two years demonstrated a positive change in either their attitudes (to school, to teachers and/ or to learning) or their behaviour (in terms of improved attendance, punctuality and/ or completion of work). This provides some quantifiable support for the view, expressed by many teachers and pupils in EIC schools, that the learning mentor strand had led to significant changes in pupil behaviour in the classroom. (Morris *et al*, 2004a: 19-23)

According to the definition of learning mentoring in chapter two (explored further in chapter 4), a primary function of learning mentors is to 'promote effective participation, enhance individual learning, raise aspirations and achieve full potential'. And participation – the many ways in which schools actively involve pupils – enjoyment of school and opportunities to contribute to society are now features of school self-evaluation and Ofsted inspections. Using case studies from the practice community, the third section of this book explores how learning mentors contribute to the capacity of schools to achieve this. Appendix A sets out how learning mentors are supporting the five *Every Child Matters* outcomes (DfES, 2004e).

Leadership and management of learning mentors in a redefined school improvement agenda

Official definitions of inclusion, with their narrow focus on 'special educational needs' and disability, are unhelpful in supporting schools to make sense of a broader inclusion agenda. If broadly conceptualised, inclusion might incorporate race equality, the Excellence in Cities programmes – plus learning mentors and so called gifted and talented provision – and other strands of support in schools that work towards increasing participation and social equality. As the number of support posts in schools increases, it becomes increasingly difficult to ensure that strands of support are complementary, rather than duplicating roles and responsibilities or support to individual pupils. Chapter four takes up this issue in greater depth, discussing how school leaders can review support structures, roles and responsibilities and develop effective tracking systems to ensure that all forms of support are complementary and contribute to equality of opportunity, in the broad context of inclusion and multi-agency working.

I have dealt with the 'why?' – the moral imperative to narrow the gap between high and low achievement and between high and low engagement in school – and identified the 'what?' – the unequal structures that create these gaps. Learning mentors are a part of the 'how'. They can make a difference at both individual and systems levels. But this is not the whole picture. Learning mentors are part of bigger policy developments in a changing children's workforce and changing social policy. Learning mentors are part of the solution, but not the whole solution. So what might the conditions be that lead to more equitable results and higher levels of pupil achievement and engagement?

Selection or the comprehensive principle – which is the real 'battering ram against inequality'?

The social democratic settlement we seek aspires to make universal the life chances of the most fortunate... In an unequal society, how can excellent provision serve the least fortunate, rather than the most? One answer is to say it cannot; excellence will always be monopolised by the well-off, so a social democratic approach should simply be to tackle poor performance. I believe this is absurdly wrong. We must tackle failure. But aside from the absurdity of trying to put a glass ceiling on

the achievement of different services, excellence can be used
as a battering ram against inequality. (Milliband, 2004: 1-2)

What kind of social democratic settlement is Milliband propos-
ing? One influenced by Charles Sabel, co-author with Michael
Piore of *The Second Industrial Divide* (1986). Milliband puts
forward a market-driven solution to social democratic settlement, arguing that if mass production is superseded in ad-
vanced economies by flexible specialisation then what we need
in public services is personalisation. Significantly, his particular
style of personalised learning is less about engaging pupils and
more about the 'consumer voice' of parents. Milliband's brand
of personalisation is therefore closely linked to selection (on the
basis of 'specialist' provision, faith schools and city academies).
It is difficult to find the hard evidence that selection will result
in a real social democratic settlement. It is comparable to the
Leave No Child Behind Act in the United States, 'in which the
federal government stated that parents of children who are
attending poorly performing schools that are not improving
can send their children to other, better-performing schools
'where practical'' (Fullan, 2003: 48). As Fullan argues, this had
no chance of changing the system and hardly any chance of
working for more than a handful of average and high socio-
economic status parents, who had the resources to exercise this
choice. Furthermore, it is likely to mean that popular schools
will become more popular with increasingly large number of
pupils from average and high socio-economic status families.

If the government is really invested in excellence and equity, in
closing the gap between the highest and lowest achievers and
achieving economic well-being for all children – a truly social
democratic settlement – it would do well to analyse the PISA
2000 evidence carefully. Evidence from PISA 2000 suggests that
pupils who attend school where there is a concentration of
pupils from low socio-economic families are less likely to
achieve and more likely to be disaffected from school. In fact,
'the socio-economic composition of a school's student population is an even stronger predictor of student performance than

individual home background' (OECD, 2001: 21). This has huge implications for policy. The PISA report suggests that educational policy 'might attempt to moderate the impact of home background on student performance by reducing the extent of segregation along socio-economic lines, or by allocating resources to schools differentially' (*ibid*).

Excellence in Cities is the government's attempt to target resources to schools differentially. This is laudable, but even this is not the whole solution, particularly if selection and instrumentalist forms of learning are actually working against narrowing the achievement gap between pupils with the highest and lowest performance. If, as PISA suggests, reducing segregation along economic lines is a way of moderating the impact of poverty, then it turns out that the comprehensive principle is the real battering ram against social inequality.

The argument for school leaders to make a difference beyond the school

Fullan's moral imperative does not stop at school improvement. He argues that school leaders need to make a significant difference at the level of systems and structures.

> At school level... the moral imperative of the principal involves leading deep cultural change that mobilises the passion and commitment of teachers, parents and others to improve the learning of all students, including closing the achievement gap. (Fullan, 2003: 41)

But, Fullan argues, the moral imperative will not amount to much unless school leaders effect system change. 'The new school leader must be fully cognisant of the big picture. The most effective leaders are those who can see and appreciate the larger context within which they operate' (Fullan, 2003: 59-60). In the current policy context, this means that school leaders will need to seize the possibilities of *Every Child Matters* and the Children Act (2004), workforce reform and Excellence in Cities to effect both structural and systems-level change. Deep change must focus on social equality, the relationships between pupils and teachers and strengthening the sense of community if the change agenda is to effect a real social democratic settlement. Learning mentors are a part of this, but can only be effective in a school culture and a children's workforce that focuses on structures and systems, and ways of learning, that promote equality. We need to avoid what Colley calls the 'impossible fiction' in which 'policies reverse the roles of structure and agency, by expecting individuals – socially excluded young people and their [learning] mentors – to create solutions to problems that are rooted in social structure' (Colley, 2003: 170). School leaders need to seize the opportunities in a climate of change and enable learning mentors to be part of a bigger structural solution to social and educational inequality.

4

Managing learning
mentor provision

This chapter returns to the issue of effective leadership and management of learning mentors in a redefined school improvement agenda. If learning mentor provision is going to be successful, it must be integrated effectively with other provision within the school.

Reviewing structures, roles and responsibilities to promote inclusion, achievement and engagement

In response to the proliferation of support roles and the requirement in both the Ofsted *Framework for Inspecting Schools* (2003b, 2005) and the *Statutory code of practice on the duty to promote race equality* (2001) to analyse and devise strategies for dealing with differences in achievement and to ensure that all groups of pupils in the school are achieving as highly as they can, some schools have created a senior leadership post with responsibility for inclusion or equality. This postholder's responsibility includes an overview of what the school is doing to raise achievement – and narrow the achievement gap between pupils with the highest and lowest attainment – and to promote participation and equality of opportunity. The postholder works to raise achievement, improve equality of opportunity and outcome for pupils and promote participation and engagement.

Schools that have achieved this successfully have generally reviewed their structures, roles and responsibilities to ensure that all strands of support complement each other. There are many ways to undertake a review of this nature. *The Index for Inclusion: developing learning and participation in schools* (CSIE, 2000) provides an excellent set of materials to support schools in undertaking this process. It is a 'systematic way of engaging in school development planning, priorities for change, implementing developments and reviewing progress' (CSIE, 2000: 7). The dimensions identified in *The Index*, help schools to consider how they can create inclusive cultures, policies and practices. Support is defined in *The Index* as 'all activities which increase the capacity of a school to respond to student diversity' (CSIE, 2000: 11). This definition supports the reframed school improvement agenda outlined in chapter two and the new inspection framework. It includes support for pupils with 'special educational needs', those with special abilities (the 'gifted and talented'), pupils using English as an additional language, pupils who are not achieving to the full, and pupils whose poor attendance restricts their learning.

Integrating learning mentor provision: understanding 'barriers to learning and participation'

The *Index* distances itself from the concept and language of special educational needs, arguing that the approach with which the discourse of special educational needs is associated 'has limitations as a way of resolving educational difficulties and can be a barrier to the development of inclusive practice in schools' (CSIE, 2000: 13). The discourse of special educational needs is located within a medical model that views difficulties as personal deficiencies. The way pupils with special educational needs are categorised separates them from pupils in mainstream education. So the Index tries to minimise the categorisation of pupils as having special educational needs, to re-frame special needs policies as inclusion policies and to ensure that support is organised for diversity.

The *Index* attempts to replace the concept special educational needs with the term 'barriers to learning and participation'. This is slightly confusing as the role of learning mentors is defined as removing barriers to learning. Does this mean that learning mentors are a resource for working with children and young people who have historically been identified as having special educational needs?

'Barriers to learning' is often used but curiously ill-defined. What does this mean? We need to explore a theory-based definition. The barriers to learning most often associated with special educational needs usually include 'biological' barriers created by a 'long term limitation of physical, intellectual or sensory function' (adapted from *Disabled People's International*, 1981, cited in CSIE, 2000: 14). Note that this is not intended to be a medical or deficit definition. Rather, difficulties are 'created by the interaction of discriminatory attitudes, actions, cultures, policies and institutional practices' (CSIE, 2000: 14).

It is this group of children and young people with 'long term limitations of physical, intellectual or sensory function' that have historically received support through 'special needs' assistants, a range of health professionals and teachers with specialist knowledge. There are also a range of support assistants, teaching assistants or learning assistants in schools, working under the direction of teachers who help to differentiate the curriculum, understanding that all pupils have different starting points in their learning. The role of these assistants is to help make changes in the teaching and learning arrangements in the classroom, required to maximise learning and participation.

For some children and young people, it is their social, emotional or behavioural development that becomes a barrier to their learning. The deficit definitions in the Education Act

(1996) and special educational needs legislation and codes of practices have created some confused and confusing thinking on this issue: somehow, 'emotional and behavioural difficulties' both are and are not special educational needs. I have analysed and problematised the history of this term elsewhere (Cruddas and Haddock, 2003). Suffice it to say that deficit definitions of 'emotional and behavioural difficulties' are unhelpful and that difficulties in social, emotional and behavioural development should not be pathologised. Neither should they be understood to be created by the attitudes, values and beliefs of pupils or families. Like the term special educational needs, it is better to replace 'emotional and behavioural difficulties' with a clearer idea of the barriers to learning and participation experienced by each individual.

It is useful to think about these barriers in the context of a child's development within the systems of relationships that form their environment. Bronfenbrenner's (1979) ecological systems theory provides a good starting point for doing this. Bronfenbrenner defines the ecological environment as a set of nested structures or systems. He examines the child's development within the context of the environment, and proposes that development can be defined as the interaction between the developing person and the environment:

> Development is defined as the person's evolving conception of the ecological environment, and his (sic) relation to it, as well as the person's growing capacity to discover, sustain, or alter its properties. (Bronfenbrenner, 1979: 9)

The innermost level is the immediate setting. This can be the home or the classroom. Bronfenbrenner regards as very important the connections between other persons present in the setting and their influence on the developing child. He calls this complex system of interrelations the microsystem. Bronfenbrenner defines the microsystem as 'a pattern of activities, roles and interpersonal relations experienced by the developing person in a given setting with particular physical and material characteristics' (1979: 22).

Bronfenbrenner proposes that this principle of interconnectedness is seen as applying not only within settings but also between settings. He calls this the 'mesosystem' (1979: 7-8). He defines the mesosystem as comprising 'the interrelations among two or more settings in which the developing person actively participates (such as, for a child, the relations among home, school and neighbourhood peer group...)' (1979:25).

He maintains that the ecological environments that impact on a developing child may include those that the child never enters, but in which events occur that affect what happens in her immediate environment. This is identified as the exosystem: 'An exosystem refers to one or more settings that do not involve the developing person as an active participant, but in which events occur that affect, or are affected by, what happens in the setting containing the developing person' (1979: 25).

Bronfenbrenner views the complex of nested, interconnected systems as a 'manifestation of overarching patterns of ideology and organisation of the social institutions common to a particular culture or subculture' (*ibid*). This he calls the macrosystem: 'The macrosystem refers to consistencies, in the form and content of lower-order systems (micro-, meso-, and exo-) that exist, or could exist, at the level of subculture or the culture as a whole, along with the belief systems or ideology underlying such consistencies' (1979: 26).

The last system in Bronfenbrenner's theory is the chronosystem: the dimension of time as it relates to the child's environments, such as the death of a parent or physiological changes that happen as children grow older.

Thus Bronfenbrenner argues for including environmental interconnections, barriers and opportunities in understanding a child's development and psychological growth. The ecological environment clearly impacts on a child's development and psychological growth, affecting cognitive, behavioural, social and emotional functioning. Sometimes difficulties in or between these systems create barriers to learning and participa-

tion at school. Thus, (as discussed in chapter nine) it is important for learning mentors to undertake ecological assessment in
order to understand each child's learning and development *in
context*.

Significantly, Bronfenbrenner argues:

> The child's evolving phenomenological world is truly a con-
> struction of reality rather than a mere representation of it... the
> child's evolving construction of reality cannot be directly
> observed; it can only be inferred from patterns of activity as
> these are expressed in both verbal and non-verbal behaviour,
> particularly in the activities, roles and relations in which the
> person engages. (1979: 10-11)

It is therefore crucial that learning mentors engage with the
child's construction of reality, including their beliefs about
themselves as learners, within the learning mentoring relationship. This is discussed in chapters seven and eight, where I look
at Egan's (2002) problem-management, opportunity-development approach to helping.

Daniels believes that it is a mistake to view the social context of
development simply as the objective environment (2001: 19),
citing in support Cole's critical engagement with Bronfenbrenner's theory:

> Cole (1996) distinguishes between notions of context defined
> as that which surrounds and notions of context defined as that
> which weaves together. In so doing, he draws on the legacy of
> Bronfenbrenner's 1979 book on the ecology of human
> development, which portrayed layers of context in concentric
> circles. This image of progressive wrapping of the individual in
> ever wider context is transformed by Cole into the following
> position: 'the combination of goals, tools and setting... con-
> stitutes simultaneously the context of behaviours and ways in
> which cognition can be related to that context' (Cole, 1996:
> 137). Here we have implications of active construction of con-
> text in action... Bronfenbrenner's 'onion rings' may be re-
> shaped, transformed, deleted and mutually interpenetrated.
> (Daniels: 2001: 19)

So it is useful to conceptualise and contextualise children's development within the interconnecting systems of relations that form their environment. But, heeding Cole's concerns, we should resist thinking of the environment as a 'package of independent variables' (Cole, 1994: 84, cited in Daniels, *op cit*). Equally, it is unhelpful to construct barriers to learning and participation as a package of independent variables. Rather, the barriers are interpenetrating and woven together and the environment is the medium, which can be re-shaped and transformed in the journey towards personal growth.

Broadly speaking, learning mentors work with children and young people who are not achieving their potential because they are experiencing difficulties in or between one or more of these systems, i.e. in the broader social and personal contexts, and this is undermining their learning and participation at school. These barriers may be internalised, taking the form of low self-esteem, lack of confidence or unmanageable feelings of anger, loss or sadness. Other barriers can be identified in external behaviours, such as aggressive, self-harming, violent or withdrawn behaviours. They may present in children's isolation from their peers or in a their affective development. They may affect attendance at school, engagement in learning, or social and emotional development.

Learning mentors' work demonstrates the connection between the social and the psychological by directly referencing the material circumstances in which barriers to learning and participation are constructed. Significantly, this way of conceptualising these barriers enables a much more complex analysis based on exclusionary pressures and unequal structures, rather than simply on the attitudes, values and beliefs of young people or their families. Chapter eight discusses an ecological model of assessment based on this broader understanding of barriers to learning and participation.

It is sometimes difficult to distinguish between low attainment due to a long-term 'learning difficulty' or 'learning disability' and pupils who are underachieving because of difficulties in their ecological environment. At the risk of stating the obvious, pupils with 'learning difficulties' may have low attainment when compared to their peers, but may be achieving as much as they are able. Underachievement refers to pupils who have the potential or ability to achieve more highly than they are. It is the latter group who are the focus of learning mentors' work. Learning mentors support the development of skills for learning for this group of pupils, increasing participation and a sense of belonging.

Many children who have long term physical, intellectual and sensory difficulties also do not achieve as much as they can because difficulties in their ecological environments hamper their learning and participation. Similarly, children for whom English is an additional language or those arriving at school mid-term may be performing below par. In these cases, it may be appropriate for a learning mentor to support the pupil, but the school should be clear about how the learning mentor's intervention is additional and different to the interventions made by other support staff.

Schools that move away from the discourses of deficit such as 'emotional and behavioural difficulties' and 'special educational needs' are more likely to have high expectations of what every pupil can achieve. And where strands of support are integrated at policy level, support functions well defined and support staff deployed in the context of increasing capacity to respond to pupil diversity, schools are more likely to be effective in creating inclusive cultures, policies and practices that support pupil engagement and achievement and therefore school improvement. In such schools, learning mentors are integral to the school's capacity to offer inclusive learning opportunities within an equal opportunities framework. Line management of learning mentors is easily identifiable and line management functions are undertaken within a broader focus on inclusion and equality.

There is no longer a statutory requirement for schools to hold a special educational needs register. In the interests of increasing capacity to respond to pupil diversity, some schools have developed inclusion registers that map support across the school and monitor and track pupils' learning and participation. Inclusion registers have the added advantage of supporting teaching and learning, as teachers can plan lessons according to the pupils' known abilities and needs, and ensure that lessons are responsive to pupil diversity.

Cohort identification

Learning mentor activity focuses on supporting achievement and engagement in the broad context of inclusion activity and multi-agency working. Thus learning mentor cohorts should consist of pupils who are experiencing barriers to learning and participation as identified through robust and accountable procedures. Schools usually have referral procedures, based on a clear understanding of pupils who consistently under perform, who are not engaged in school life because their poor attendance is a barrier to their learning or because their sense of belonging to the school community is weak and who may be experiencing difficulties in their ecological environments.

Procedures for identifying this group vary. Some schools use performance and tracking data – including national curriculum levels and standardised test results – teacher assessment, attendance data, behaviour tracking data, information from parents, and a knowledge and understanding of what is happening in their wider ecological environments. Some schools also offer a procedure for pupils to self-refer, respecting the understanding children themselves have of their own barriers to learning and participation, and their willingness to change.

It is useful for schools to have a 'learning discussion' in the context of a professional development or staff meeting about what is meant by underachievement. If teachers were asked to describe a pupil who is underachieving, what might they say? What evidence might they give? It is also helpful to consider what factors might mask underachievement. Schools are getting better at identifying 'invisible' underachievers by using jagged profiles. A jagged profile describes differences in attainment scores, which should be similar. For example, spelling age and reading age or non-verbal and verbal scores on standardised tests. Jagged profiles can help identify pupils who are or are likely to achieve below their capacity. Other indicators are significant changes in their social or emotional behaviour, learning behaviour and participation.

School leaders and managers may wish to consider how school monitoring systems support and encourage teachers to think about underachievement and how referral forms and processes might help them think about who might be underachieving.

Whatever procedure is used in a school to identify underachievement, it should be clear to all staff, parents and pupils. Referral procedures, criteria and roles and responsibilities are usually written into a school policy – either a discrete learning mentor policy, or a more generic inclusion or equality and diversity policy that includes learning mentor functions.

Line managing learning mentor provision

Line management of learning mentors should be clearly identified. Because learning mentors carry out much of their work in a one-to-one context, they should have regular and dedicated opportunities to meet with their line manager, to reflect on their practice and ensure that it is safe. This meeting time should be guaranteed and records kept of the meetings. Line managers support learning mentor work by undertaking regular caseload review, including supervision for particular cases. Line managers also support learning mentors in planning their work and time-tabling.

Monitoring and evaluating learning mentor provision

The *Value Base*, published alongside the *National Occupational Standards for Learning, Development and Support Services* (ENTO, PAULO and TOPSS, 2003b) states that 'A key aspect of professional practice is a reflection of own contribution to the quality of service provision'. Increasingly, schools are including learning mentors in performance management arrangements. Performance review or appraisal provides the opportunity for learning mentors and their line managers to undertake a structured enquiry into how practice can be developed.

Regular line management meetings and performance review are key to sustaining and enhancing professional practice. However, schools also need to evaluate learning mentor provision. There are a variety of ways in which this can be done, from quality assured audits to the analysis of quantitative and qualitative data. A range of techniques can be used to gather qualitative and quantitative data: the pupils' opinions, staff and parent perceptions, observations, measuring progress against individual targets and case studies.

Learning mentors in schools usually agree with their line managers about what achievement and engagement baseline and outcome data will be collected at individual pupil level, and then analysed and interpreted. These data contribute to and enhance other data schools collect. Quantitative data give important evidence of the impact of learning mentor provision but they cannot provide the whole picture. Qualitative data and softer data are arguably more important indicators of the impact of this provision. There is now much greater emphasis on the right of pupils to have a voice and to influence service provision. Ofsted inspections will increasingly focus on the experiences of pupils in schools, and case studies will be acceptable evidence.

Fundamental to any evaluation or analysis of impact are the views of the pupils and their families. It is increasingly expected that the views of pupils and their families should be used to inform and improve service delivery. Learning mentors can use these data to provide an annual report or to contribute to a report on the overall impact of strategies to promote inclusion. The data should also be used to determine priorities for development and included in the school or department's improvement plan.

Preparing for inspections in the context of continuous self-evaluation

Ofsted is increasingly focusing on learning mentor provision during inspections. Her Majesty's Inspector, David Moore prepared a sample briefing paper to guide schools on how learning mentors and their line managers can prepare for inspections, in the context of continuous self-evaluation. The following is an example of how one school interpreted Moore's guidance and created their own briefing paper.

Case study 2: Greenleaf Primary School's briefing paper for Ofsted

The school receives EIC funding for one LM. The LM has a precise job description.

The LM is managed by a member of the senior management team, who is also responsible for other inclusion initiatives in the school. The LM is included in the school's performance management arrangements. Development priorities have been identified in the LM Action Plan. These are reflected in the School Improvement Plan.

The school has devised criteria for referral, length of intervention and its nature. Information about learning mentoring is displayed on a notice board in the staff room and is included in the staff handbook. At the start of every term, supply cover is provided for teachers who are released to review referrals to the LM and discuss new referrals. Referral forms are kept in the staff room where they are easily accessible to staff. Referrals are discussed during a caseload management session with the line manager.

The school also has a LM Policy, setting out aims of the programme, key roles and responsibilities. This policy has been discussed with staff at a meeting in October 2003, at which the LM gave a short INSET on his role and staff had an opportunity to discuss caseload and mentee data.

The average caseload for one-to-one mentoring work at any point in time is fifteen pupils. The caseload includes pupils on short-term, medium-term and longer-term intervention. After six weeks of establishing a relationship of trust, Individual Action Plans are written with pupils and parents (where possible) and targets are set. The Individual Action Plans are then distributed to class teachers, parents and to the LM's line manager. Pupils are mentored for one term in the first instance, prior to review.

The LM also runs four groups:

Two confidence and self-esteem building groups

Two motivation groups

In each case, groups are run for Years 5 and 6 and for Years 3 and 4, targeting six pupils in each group. The groups are run once a week on a circle time model. Some innovative project work is undertaken in the groups, for example a digital video story around confidence and self-esteem.

The LM runs out of hours learning sessions, including:

A running club on Mondays for pupils in Years 5 and 6 and on Wednesdays for pupils in Years 3 and 4, supporting approximately twenty pupils in total, promoting attendance and punctuality, health and well-being and providing a positive start to the day.

A chess club on Monday lunchtimes for pupils in Years 5 and 6 targeting ten pupils.

A football club on Mondays after school for Year 6 targeting approximately thirty pupils (boys and girls).

A fun club on Tuesday lunchtimes for Years 5 and 6 and Thursday lunchtimes for Years 3 and 4, targeting approximately thirty pupils per session. This is aimed at pupils who are vulnerable in the playground. Structured play and co-operative games are provided.

The LM's work impacts on the whole school. The LM has an important role in transfer and transition and has developed good links with partner secondary schools to support pupils at the point of transfer to secondary school. An innovative digital video interface project was piloted with two local secondary schools. The whole Year 6 group were involved in this project. Each pupil had three questions that they asked. An edited version was then discussed with Year 7 pupils (formerly from Greenleaf so that they were 'recognisable faces'). The Year 7 pupils' responses were filmed and the footage was edited at the City Learning Centre by Year 6 pupils.

The LM has also arranged for a senior teacher from a partner secondary school, accompanied by two former Greenleaf pupils, to visit and talk to the Year 6 group about transfer to secondary.

The LM works in partnership with the PSHE co-ordinator to deliver the Sex and Relationship module of the PSHE curriculum.

The LM also runs the school council in partnership with his line manager. A council meeting is held once a week at which councillors (in Year 6) discuss issues to do with the school. Councillors also do duties around the school and this is overseen by the LM.

The LM also has responsibility for school's sport strategy. He co-ordinates all the sporting events.

The LM also has a role monitoring attendance and lateness. Parents or carers are contacted on first day unauthorised absences, lateness is monitored on a weekly basis and after two late registrations, the family is contacted. The LM invites parents in to discuss their child's attendance and how the school can best support them. The LM liases with the school nurse and Education Welfare Officer (EWO) on a weekly basis to discuss concerns or referrals for chronic lateness and poor attendance.

The school sets great store by its links with parents and the wider community. The LM communicates regularly with parents of pupils on his caseload by telephone calls, meetings and informal discussion. Parents and carers whose child has been referred to a LM receive a letter inviting them to a meeting to discuss this support.

The LM has worked with the Community Learning and Skills Service to oversee family learning programmes within the school. A 'Keeping up with the Children' numeracy programme was run over 6 weeks for parents, introducing them to key ideas from the National Numeracy Strategy and providing methods to support their children's learning. A maths workshop was also run for parents with children in nursery and reception.

The school has defined the LMs' role as supporting pupils in overcoming barriers to learning. The school has adopted the EIC Partnership's Monitoring and Evaluation Strategy. Termly surveys were completed over the last academic year to monitor and track individual pupil progress. The school has participated in self-evaluation using the DfES LM Audit Instrument.

In the last academic year the LM has supported 23 pupils on a one-to-one basis. The breakdown of referrals (by primary reason for referral) is:

Seventeen pupils referred for issues related to learning;

Four pupils referred for issue related to social, emotional and behavioural development

One pupil referred for issues related to attendance and punctuality

The average length of time that a LM sees a pupil over a week is forty minutes in one-to-one sessions.

Outcomes at the point of data collection:

88 percent of pupils referred for issues related to their learning, reported improvements in their learning, mostly related to improvements in attitude to learning, raised expectations and improved confidence.

Two of the four pupils referred for issues relating to social, emotional and behavioural development showed improvement in these areas and the other two pupils demonstrated raised expectations and improved confidence.

The pupil referred for issues related to attendance and punctuality showed improvements in these areas.

The documents referred to in the briefing paper were compiled in an evidence folder, in preparation for the inspection.

Inspectors considered the learning mentor practice at this school to be 'outstanding'. The registered inspector commented in the Ofsted report: 'The work of the Learning Mentor is outstanding and helps specific groups of pupils to develop self-confidence, think better of themselves and where necessary, to improve their behaviour.'

It is clear from this briefing paper that the learning mentor at Greenleaf Primary School is helping the school to deliver the five key *Every Child Matters* outcomes: staying healthy, enjoying and achieving, keeping safe, contributing to the community and achieving social and economic well-being. The learning mentor helps children to be healthy by promoting healthy lifestyles through his out of school-hours clubs and activities. His work in co-delivering the PSHE curriculum, particularly the module on sex and relationships, helps children make choices that keep them safe. All his work helps the pupils to enjoy and achieve. He works with children and families to support attendance at school and his one-to-one and group work supports children's personal, social and emotional development. His family learning programmes help parents and carers to support their children to enjoy and achieve at school. His work in supporting the school council helps children to make a positive contribution to their school and participate in decision-making. Helping children make a positive contribution is also about managing change and responding to challenges – this is done effectively by supporting transfer and transition. The extent to which learners enjoy and achieve, adopt safe practices and healthy lifestyles and are able to make a positive contribution all make a difference to their life chances and ability to achieve economic well-being.

From September 2005, school inspections will evaluate the extent to which schools are supporting the five *Every Child Matters* outcomes (see Appendix A). Schools will have to provide evidence of how they are doing this through self-evaluation. The following section sets out the key questions in the new *Framework for Inspecting Schools* (Ofsted, 2005).

How well do learners achieve?

Inspectors' responsibilities include evaluating and reporting on the learners' success in achieving their learning goals, trends over time and any significant variations between groups of learners. Inspectors will also evaluate the development of skills that contribute to social and economic well-being, the behaviour and attendance of learners and the extent to which they adopt safe practices and healthy lifestyles.

Learning mentors are an important part of a school's resources in addressing inequality related to the gap in attainment between the highest and lowest performance (see chapter three). They have a key role in the way the school provides for all its pupils, ensuring that all pupils are achieving to the full and derive maximum benefit from all that is on offer. Learning mentors are not responsible for the content of the curriculum. They stimulate the desire to learn and create opportunities for personal growth through a working alliance. Their role is defined as facilitating access to learning by helping to dismantle barriers to learning and participation and to develop the skills for learning.

The barriers to learning and participation that pupils experience may be relationship barriers: relationships with peers, school staff or family. Learning mentors help pupils understand these relationships better, make sense of what is going on and seek solutions that make sense for them. They can be part of the way the school promotes good behaviour and social well-being.

Many learning mentors also implement specific programmes to ensure good relationships among peers, for example, peer buddying and peer mentoring programmes as described in chapter nine.

Learning mentors have a key role in supporting attendance and engagement at school. Many learning mentors meet regularly with the school's Education Welfare Officer to discuss strategies and support each other's work.

Learning mentors also seek to understand and engage with the broader environments in which the pupil functions, including home, school and community. In this way, they are essential to keeping children safe.

How effective are teaching, training and learning?

Inspectors must evaluate the suitability and rigour of assessment in planning and monitoring learners' progress, the provision for additional learning needs and the involvement of parents and carers in their children's learning and development.

Learning mentors facilitate access to learning for pupils who are experiencing barriers to learning. An essential part of the process of learning mentoring is assessment of need and rigorous action planning (see chapter eight).

Learning mentors also have a key role in parental liaison and work with families. They maintain close contact with the families of children and young people on their caseloads. They can also run parent groups through informal coffee mornings and sometimes more structured courses to help parents support their children's learning more effectively or to seek parents' views (see chapter ten).

How well do programmes and activities meet the needs and interests of learners?

Inspectors are responsible for evaluating and reporting on whether programmes and activities match learners' aspirations and potential, how far these programmes are responsive to local circumstances and how enrichment activities or other extended services contribute to learners' enjoyment and achievement.

As noted, learning mentors are not part of the delivery of the content of the curriculum, but rather facilitate access to learning by helping to dismantle barriers to learning and participation. They can provide support outside the school day which is responsive to local circumstances: breakfast clubs, homework clubs and a variety of clubs promoting participation in sport, the arts and other interests. Learning mentors thus contribute to the capacity of a school to offer extended services and enrichment outside of school hours.

How well are learners guided and supported?

Inspectors must evaluate and report on care, advice, guidance and other support provided to safeguard welfare, promote personal development and achieve high standards. They must evaluate the extent to which the provision contributes to the learners' capacity to stay safe and healthy.

Learning mentors provide support and guidance to pupils by using person-centred, problem management and opportunity approaches. They implement strategies to ensure that the school seeks, values and acts on children and young people's views by, for example, managing the school council.

How effective are leadership and management in raising achievement and supporting all learners?

Inspectors evaluate a number of leadership roles in this area, including how effective the links are with other providers, services and organisations to promote the integration of care, education and any other extended services in schools to enhance learning.

As part of the broader children's workforce, learning mentors are at the vanguard of change in schools. They already work within an extended range of networks, developing effective working partnerships with other agencies and supporting multi-agency working.

This chapter has considered how learning mentors can be integrated effectively with other provision within the school. Building on the analysis of how learning mentors contribute to school improvement, it showed how schools can evaluate learning mentor provision and prepare for school inspections. To repeat: learning mentors' work should not be constituted in, or constrained by, the standards agenda. They contribute to narrowing the gap between achievement and engagement by working within a transitive and social model of learning. This claim needs to be explored in more detail, looking at theories that anchor learning mentor practice and working towards a model of learning mentoring. This is the focus of the next section of this book, beginning with determining a functional definition of learning mentoring.

PART TWO
TOWARDS A THEORY-BASED MODEL
OF LEARNING MENTORING

5

A functional definition of learning mentor practice – towards person-centred practice

The last three chapters sought to locate learning mentoring in a policy context and within the broader context of school improvement. This chapter works towards a functional definition of learning mentoring so as to locate it within a broader theoretical position: as person-centred and democratic education.

Commissioning functional mapping

In 2001, the Connexions Service National Unit commissioned the national training organisation for community-based learning in the United Kingdom (PAULO) to develop National Occupational Standards for the Connexions Service. The scope of this project was then extended to include Learning Mentors and the Education Welfare Service (and two other national training organisations, ENTO and TOPSS were brought on board). The first phase of the project was a functional mapping exercise of each of the three services, undertaken with the support of Sauvé Bell Associates, through extensive national consultation with the practice community. *A Functional Map for the Provision of Learning Mentor Services* was finalised in May 2003.

Colley points out that researchers have tried to define mentoring in terms of mentor functions and is critical of such analyses of mentor functions, because mentoring is practised in many different contexts:

> If we defined mentoring by its functions, it would create an effect similar to the *lipsmackinthirstquenchinacetastinmotivatingoodbuzzincooltalkinhighwalkinfastlivinevergivencoolfizzen.* ... Pepsi-Cola advertisement. We would find ourselves confronted with a litany of mentoring functions that may never be exhaustive: teaching, coaching, advising, guiding, directing, protecting, supporting, sponsoring, challenging, encouraging, motivating, befriending, inspiring, *esteembuildinrolemodellin informationgivinskillsharincareerdevelopinnovicenurturinriskt akingradimprovinaspirationraisinhorizenbroadenintargetsettin kingmakinselfregeratincriticallyreflectinperformancassessinfee dbackgivin...* (Colley, 2003: 31)

Colley's analysis of mentoring is firmly located in volunteer mentor programmes. The plethora of volunteer mentoring programmes in different contexts may indeed have resulted in a 'litany' of mentoring functions. So surely it is important that learning mentoring is properly and rigorously defined in terms of its functions. How else are we to avoid the pitfalls of learning mentoring meaning all things to all people? Functional mapping becomes a set of descriptive boundaries.

A functional definition of learning mentoring

The *Functional Map for the Provision of Learning Mentor Services* defines learning mentoring as:

> [providing] support and guidance to children, young people and those engaged with them, by removing barriers to learning in order to promote effective participation, enhance individual learning, raise aspirations and achieve full potential. (Sauvé Bell: 2003)

It is worth considering this definition in some detail. Learning mentoring is described as providing 'support and guidance'. We saw how learning mentors fit into the broader children's workforce: professionals including learning mentors, education welfare officers, personal advisors, health, social services and others working in a multi-agency context to improve children's life chances, including their engagement with learning. The support and guidance function performed by learning mentors make them entirely different from other support roles within schools, for example, teaching assistants. Whereas teaching assistants work under the direction of teachers to support teaching and learning in the context of the curriculum, learning mentors support pupils to access learning. This distinction is crucial. As the schools' workforce changes under the remodelling agenda and more professionals are working in schools as part of the broader children's workforce, school leaders will need to ensure that structures within schools provide complementary services.

The purpose of a learning mentor's intervention with a pupil is to *remove barriers to learning.* A theoretical definition of barriers to learning has located this term in Bronfenbrenner's ecological systems theory (see chapter three). Difficulties in or between the ecological systems can create barriers to learning and participation that are internalised by the pupil. The messages about 'self' they receive in the ecological systems can lead to psychological, emotional, social and behavioural barriers. In establishing supportive relationships, whether one-to-one or in groups, the role of the learning mentor is to remove these barriers. Chapter eight draws heavily on Gerard Egan's (2002) work about a model of helping, to explain how skilled learning mentors engage in supportive relationships, not only to remove barriers and manage problems but also to create opportunities, using the skills and personal resources children bring to the process.

If we accept ecological systems theory as a way of understanding what barriers to learning might mean – heeding Daniel's caution that it is a mistake to view the social context of development simply as the objective environment – learning mentors should also work with many of the people who are part of the broader systems that define a child's world. The functional definition states that learning mentors 'provide support and guidance to children, young people *and those engaged with them*' (my italics). Learning mentors work within an extended range of networks to support individual pupils on their case-loads: school staff, peers, families and statutory and voluntary agencies who are involved with them or the family. So although school-based, learning mentors do not only work in schools: they work to dismantle barriers and decrease exclusionary pressures in the broader systems that define the child's world. They also broker support and learning opportunities and help to improve the quality of services to children and families.

Working within the larger ecological systems locates the work of learning mentors within the broader nature of schools as institutions. Learning mentors adopt a 'problem-management, opportunity development' approach (Egan, 2002) to helping children overcome barriers. They adopt the same approach to dismantling institutional barriers. Thus learning mentors have a bigger and highly significant role in changing institutions. An example might be establishing a breakfast club to support attendance and give pupils a healthy start to the day. Or to change and influence playground provision so that break and lunch times are not institutional barriers to children's parti-cipation.

If the purpose of a learning mentor's intervention with a pupil is to remove barriers to learning in the ways described, the aims of learning mentoring in the functional definition must be to 'promote effective participation, enhance individual learning, raise aspirations and achieve full potential'.

The thematic report from PISA highlighted how a sense of be-longing and participation in school are important educational outcomes in their own right. Learning mentors use a skilled helping approach to support children's sense of belonging, and hence their participation in school life.

Learning mentors also aim to enhance individual learning. If, as suggested in chapter two, learning mentors are not part of the delivery of the content of the curriculum, then how do they enhance individual learning? Learning mentors, in the words of Rogers and Freiberg, provide 'the interpersonal relationship in the facilitation of learning' (1994: 151).

Rogers and Freiberg propose that 'the facilitation of significant learning rests upon certain attitudinal qualities that exist in the personal relationship between the facilitator and the learner' (1994: 153). In a climate where class sizes sometimes exceed thirty pupils to one teacher, some pupils need to experience such a personal relationship in order to access learning. My friend and colleague, Sandy Posnikoff, believes that the most important thing learning mentors bring to their work is themselves. The relationships learning mentors form with the children they work with are the crucial foundation of the facilitation of significant learning. Prizing, acceptance, trust and empathic understanding (Rogers and Freiberg, 1994: 156-157) are the qualities learning mentors bring to their professional relationships. This is not to devalue the teaching relationship. Most teachers value the interpersonal relationships they have with children and young people in their classrooms. They too prize, accept, trust and understand their pupils. Many teachers extend themselves far beyond the call of duty to form such relationships with individual pupils. What is being proposed here is that some pupils need a one-to-one relationship in order to discover themselves as learners. Learning mentors have the privilege of being employed in dedicated posts to offer this service, to help pupils access the learning environment in the classroom.

According to our functional definition, the aim of learning mentors' work is to promote effective participation and enhance individual learning. They also aim to raise aspirations and help children to achieve their potential. The functional definition actually states 'achieve their *full* potential'. While this may be a highly desirable outcome, it is perhaps unlikely that a pupil can be considered to have achieved their full potential. Ignoring the tautology, how is it possible to measure full potential? How would we account for the potential for development and growth beyond the present moment?

Perhaps this aim is best re-framed in Roger and Freiberg's terms: 'the person is the theoretical goal, the end point of personal growth' (1994: 327). A longer excerpt from Rogers and Freiberg contextualises this aim:

> Here, then, is my theoretical model of the person who emerges from ... the best of education, the individual who has experienced optimal psychological growth: a person functioning freely in all the fullness of the organismic potentialities; a person who is dependable in being realistic, self-enhancing, socialised, and appropriate in behaviour; a creative person whose specific formings of behaviour are not easily predictable; a person who is ever-changing, ever developing, always discovering the newness in each succeeding moment of time. The person is the theoretical goal, the end point of personal growth. We see persons *moving in this direction* from the best experiences in education... from the best of family and group relationships. But what we observe is the imperfect person moving towards this goal. (1994: 327)

Raising aspirations and working in the difficult and shifting sands of 'potential' is not only about supporting working class children to get good grades and go to university (although it may be this too). It is not purely instrumental, or driven by attainment outcomes. The work of learning mentors is person-centred: it is about supporting and guiding children and young people to move in the direction of personal growth.

The government's 'personalised learning' agenda has been analysed (see chapter two). On first reading, the concept of personalising learning is to be welcomed but a closer reading leads us to question where the 'person' in 'personalisation' is. Person-centred practice gives us back the person in 'personalised learning'.

The functional definition provides a starting point for considering how learning mentor practice is located in theory. This discussion draws on a person-centred perspective. Before considering other theories that can usefully be discussed, I briefly consider how 'knowledge and understanding' is constructed in the *National Occupational Standards for Learning, Development and Support Services* (ENTO, PAULO and TOPSS, 2003a) because these knowledge requirements will be used to develop qualifications.

Making the case for locating practice in theory
Exploring 'knowledge and understanding' as defined in the National Occupational Standards

The *National Occupational Standards* were developed from the functional mapping of three services: learning mentors, education welfare service and Connexions. The standards describe elements of competence and the knowledge and understanding underpinning the competences. Qualifications are in development so we should take a closer look at the knowledge requirements as they are set out in unit nine of the standards: 'facilitating children and young people's learning and development through mentoring'.

We need a definition of knowledge and understanding so we can critically engage with the definition. The standard claims that the practitioner will need the following knowledge and understanding about working with children and young people:

> Strategies for effective communication and negotiation: how to give constructive feedback; what active listening is and what barriers to child/ young person's expression may exist
>
> Learning styles and methods – what these are and how they differ between children and young people, ways of identifying child/young person's learning needs, styles and methods
>
> How bias and stereotyping may occur within the learning and mentoring process; ways of combating them; impact of own attitudes, values and behaviour on work with children and

young people and methods of monitoring that are not adversely affecting work with children and young people

Methods for encouraging and maintaining child/ young person's motivation and self-esteem; ways to adapt approaches to meet the needs of the child/ young person; problem solving techniques such as lateral thinking, how to use them and how to encourage children and young people to develop these skills themselves

Children and young people's rights within the mentoring process (to confidentiality, to make decisions etc) and how to monitor that these are upheld

How to assist children and young people's decision making in ways that promote the child/ young person's autonomy; factors and pressures which impact on children and young people's ability to make informed decisions; the range of relevant sources of information which can be accessed to support and assist children and young people; factors which may affect ability to access information

Formats for action plans, how to make action plans SMART (specific, measurable, achievable realistic, time-bound); how prior achievements, experience and learning may influence current and future choices; methods of assessing realistic rates of progress and timescales for course of action, how to encourage children and young people to review their plans in a way that encourages them to be realistic

Methods of reviewing and evaluating the effectiveness of mentoring, ways of effectively involving children and young people in the process. (ENTO, PAULO and TOPSS, 2003a)

It is interesting that this unit was developed from unit E314 of the national occupational standards for community justice. The national training organisations who developed the standards state that this standard 'has been tailored to remove all references to offending behaviour and fit the context of these standards'. And yet a narrow, instrumentalist – arguably, punitive; definitely diminishing – view of practice is retained. There is no acknowledgement of how knowledge is located in theoretical positions or how the meaning of learning is configured in engaging in the community of learning mentor practice. Knowledge, as it is constructed in the standard, appears to be a universal constant, not a deeply contested site which is linked to power relations.

The definition of knowledge raises more questions than it answers. For example, what constitutes effective communication? An adult who shouts at children, admonishing them for their behaviour, is undoubtedly communicating with them, but the communication is unhelpful, demeaning and disrespectful. However, this communication may be perceived as effective if it results in the children's compliance. But in person-centred practice, this would clearly not count as effective communication.

What is meant by 'learning styles and methods?' There is a received, rather tired, body of work in this area but no reference to a theory, so it remains unclear what 'learning styles' might mean, and to whom. Further, learning styles ignore the cultural and historical circumstances in which learning occurs (Reynolds, 1997, cited in Grey, 2001: 14).

The notion that bias and stereotyping may occur within the learning and mentoring process is important. But we need to interrogate what bias and stereotyping may mean within different theoretical and political positions. Radical, emancipatory theory argues that schools are inherently biased places since they reproduce class and culture (*inter alia* Aronowitz and Giroux, 1991, Bourdieu and Passeron,1970, Apple, 1990). Can we therefore assume that learning mentors are expected to know and understand how to combat the disenfranchising effects of schooling? Methods for encouraging and maintaining pupils' motivation and self-esteem are similarly unaffiliated to any theoretical position.

Children and young people's rights are paramount, but the examples of these rights to confidentiality and to make decisions, while important, are so obvious as to be banal. What do children's rights really mean in the context of mentoring? Do pupils have the right to make a genuine choice about learning mentoring? Do they have the right to repudiate the national curriculum that simply reproduces social hegemony and an economically stratified and segregated society?

From a unlocated bullet-point about rights, the knowledge requirements move on to an instrumentalist notion of action planning, which is not embedded in any understanding of assessment or intervention planning that would meaningfully lead to an action plan.

Much more needs to be done to build the qualifications around knowledge requirements linked to a range of theoretical models that inform practice, and a model of learning that is transitive, focused on the experiences, skills and knowledge that practitioners bring to the learning process. *The Functional Map for the Provision Learning Mentor Services*, provides a somewhat better starting point for locating learning mentor practice within theoretical models. Accordingly, this chapter has analysed a functional definition of learning mentoring so as to locate it within a broader theoretical position: person-centred and democratic education.

Part three of this book returns to the functional map of learning mentor services, expanding on this definition and exploring the functions that describe learning mentor practice in ever-greater detail. These functions are illustrated with case studies from the community of practice.

The next chapter revisits the professional groups in Europe and North America that have close competence links with learning mentors, in an attempt to learn from these professions about the bodies of knowledge and theories that inform their practice.

6

Theoretical anchors: Learning from theoretical models informing practice in the international context

In the preface to her book, Colley writes:

> Yet, as I began to study mentoring, I was shocked to realise how little evidence there is for this practice, and how flimsy its theoretical base. My own professional training in guidance allowed me to develop my practice through a range of theoretical models, and through insights into the social and economic context of careers work. I knew the same was true of youth workers in their field. Mentoring seems to lack such anchors... (2003: xiv)

Colley's analysis of mentoring, as we have noted, is firmly located within volunteer mentoring programmes seeking to re-engage young people with formal education, training and employment. However, learning mentoring, as a fledgling profession in a changing children's workforce, appears to lack the theoretical anchors described by Colley.

The functional definition explored in the last chapter leads us towards locating learning mentor practice in person-centred theory. However, ecological systems theory helps in defining 'barriers to learning' (see chapter four). Here then is another theoretical anchor. Egan's (2002) 'problem-management, opportunity-development' model of skilled helping, mentioned in the last chapter, is given careful consideration in chapter eight. It anchors learning mentor practice within person-centred theory and positive psychology. There is thus more than one theoretical anchor to apply to our model of learning mentor practice. By returning to the international perspective and seeing how the European tradition of social pedagogy and the North American profession of Child and Youth Care locate their practice in theories, we can build a rich picture of the many possible theoretical anchors for learning mentor practice.

Social pedagogy, social education, community and democracy

Learning mentoring has close occupational competence links with the European tradition of social pedagogy. Social pedagogy has a long and contested history in Europe, but its endur-ing theoretical anchors are to a body of work that stresses that learning is a social activity, intimately connected to participation in community life. One of the theoretical anchors is John Dewey's theory of democracy and education (1916).

Dewey was writing at the turn of the century at a time when several educationalists and theorists were interested in social education. Dewey wished to develop a child-centred theory but, as Smith observes, 'he added to this a powerful dimension (and one that connects with the concerns of many early champions of social pedagogy) – that the experience required for learning was participation in community life' (1999: 6). Dewey argues that education is a social function and furthermore, that education is 'a fostering, a nurturing, a cultivating process. These words all imply attention to the conditions of growth' (Dewey, 1916: 10). It is clear that Dewey links the primary purpose of education directly to personal growth.

Significantly, Dewey cautions against separating the acquisition of literacy and the content of education from the acquisition of the interests, culture and social aspects of life. He argues that such separation is avoided in education systems 'where learning is the accompaniment of continuous activities or occupations which have a social aim and utilise the materials of typical social situations. ... All education which develops the power to share effectively in social life is moral' (Dewey, 1916: 288).

Analysing what the democratic concept in education might mean, Dewey asserts that society can mean many things.

> In order to have a large number of values in common, all the members of the group must have an equable opportunity to receive and to take from others. There must be a large variety of shared understandings and experiences. Otherwise, the influences which educate some into masters, educate others into slaves. (Dewey, 1916: 69)

Dewey defines the criteria for the democratic ideal as the conditions that create 'more numerous and more varied points of shared common interest' and 'freer interaction between social groups... [the] continuous re-adjustment through meeting the new situations produced by various intercourse' (1916: 71). From this perspective social pedagogy – and learning mentoring – is about 'widening the area of shared concerns, and the liberation of a greater diversity of personal capacities' (Dewey, 1916: 71).

There are close theoretical links between Dewey's ideas of education as social practice and Vygotsky's. Daniels cites Popkewitz (1998) who analyses the similar socio-political contexts of intense modernisation which shaped the ideas of both Vygotsky and Dewey. For both, learning is conditional and contingent, shaped by particular social circumstances (Daniels, 2001: 5).

Vygotsky argued that social interaction plays a critical role in the development of cognition.

> Every function in the child's cultural development appears twice: first, on the social level, and later, on the individual level; first between people (interpsychological) and then inside the child (intrapsychological). This applies equally to voluntary

> attention, to logical memory and to the formation of concepts. All the higher functions originate as actual relationships between individuals. (Vygotsky 1978: 57)

In other words, adults are the facilitators of learning, in a social setting. So how did Vygotsky see learning happening within what he called the 'zone of proximal development'? He defined the zone of proximal development as

> ...actual development level as determined by independent problem solving and the higher level of potential development as determined through problem solving under adult guidance or in collaboration with more capable peers. (Vygotsky, 1978: 86)

Learning, in Vygotsky's view, can thus never be the narrow instrumentalist concept driven by demonstrated levels of attainment. Learning is about the potential that young people bring with them to the learning situation, how this potential is recognised and explored through problem solving, and how *control is transferred to the learner.* It is vital for social pedagogues, and for learning mentors, that their working alliance 'should create the possibilities for development, through the kind of active participation that characterises collaboration, that it should be socially negotiated and that it should entail transfer of control to the learner' (Daniels, 2001: 61). The third section of this book describes case studies from the community of practice and looks at how learning mentors support learning by recognising potential and enabling participation.

If, as Vygotsky believed, learning originates as actual relationships between people, then social learning and social development theory can support children and young people develop the skills for learning.

Social learning and social development theories have strong connections with situated learning theory, to which Lave and Wenger are important contributors. Daniels maintains that Lave and Wenger's situated learning theory is part of what could be called post-Vygotskian studies (2001: 69).

In the introduction to *Situated learning: legitimate peripheral participation*, Hanks proposes that situated learning

> ...takes as its focus the relationship between learning and the social situations in which it occurs. Rather than defining it as the acquisition of propositional knowledge, Lave and Wenger situate learning in certain forms of social co-participation. Rather than asking what kinds of cognitive processes and conceptual structures are involved, they ask what kinds of social engagements provide the proper context for learning to take place. (Hanks, in Lave and Wenger, 1991: 14)

Social pedagogues or *educateurs* create social engagements that enable learning to take place. So do learning mentors. They seek out and enable the learning in social activity but, equally, the social activity in learning.

Child and Youth Care and the psychoeducational model

Child and Youth Care work in North America has explored many different theoretical anchors. Out of them has come the psychoeducational model. The psychoeducational model is fully explored in the context of Child and Youth Care by Brendtro and Ness. Like Egan's model, the psychoeducational model is eclectic and holistic, drawing techniques from other models and theories.

> The term psychoeducational accents the close connection between education, the teaching of human beings, and psychology, the study of human behaviour (Fagen, Long and Stephens, 1975). It is neither pathology-orientated, nor exclusively behavioural, cognitive or affective in focus. (Brendtro and Ness: 1983: 16)

According to Brendtro and Ness, the psychoeducational model, although eclectic in approach, yields six tenets. I will build on these tenets to develop a working model of learning mentoring. The six tenets (defined by Brendtro and Ness, 1983: 17-24) are: relationship is primary; assessment is ecological; behaviour is holistic, teaching is humanistic; crisis is opportunity and practice is pragmatic.

Relationship is primary

Brendtro and Ness argue that 'the quality of human relation-ships is the most powerful determinant of successful pro-grammes ... methodology is less important than relationships' (1987: 17). Egan, however, in his exploration of the helping relationships, positions this view as one of three alternative views of the relationship between helper and client. He points out that some theories stress the relationship itself, others high-light the work that is to be done through the relationship and yet another group of theories focus on the outcomes to be achieved (2002: 42).

One of the dangers inherent in the first view – the relationship-in-itself which assumes that the helping is the interpersonal relationship – is the issue of professional boundaries. The help-ing relationship is *facilitative*. Too much focus on the relation-ship can lead to dependence and transference, such that the helping relationship itself becomes the 'problem'. Egan cautions that 'overstressing the relationship is a mistake be-cause it obscures the primary goal of helping a client manage a particular problem better' (2002:17).

In the second view, which highlights the work to be done through the relationship, the relationship is seen as the means to an end (Egan, 2002: 42). Proponents of this view tend to locate their practice in behavioural and cognitive theories. The third view Egan explores is that the relationship is driven by outcomes. This is very much the view of solution-focused brief therapy. A possible difficulty with both these views is that the relationship is seen as instrumental. An instrumental relation-ship can lead to unequal power relations in which the adult behaves in non-authentic ways in service of instilling institu-tional goals in young people.

Egan brings together the best of 'relationship-in-itself, relation-ship-as-means and solution-focused approaches in 'the relationship as working alliance' (2002: 43). This integrated view focuses on the collaborative nature of helping; the relationship as a forum for re-learning and relationship flexibility (Egan, 2002: 43-44). The relationship as working alliance is discussed in the next chapter.

Assessment is ecological

Brendtro and Ness propose that 'behaviour must be understood as part of the child's life-space, which includes the transactions between the child and adults, peers, task and educational system' (1987: 18). We saw in chapter four that ecological systems theory provides a useful way to understand the term barriers to learning. Ecological assessment is examined in chapter eight and highlighted with a case study from the community of practice and current policy directions.

Behaviour is holistic

As Brendtro and Ness suggest:

> Understanding behaviour requires an awareness of the cognitive, affective and motivational processes in the child and in oneself...The complex problems of children do not neatly fit the narrow professional skills of any single discipline. A cross-disciplinary approach is needed to achieve a holistic understanding of behaviour. (1983: 20)

Behaviour needs to be understood in a developmental context. Adult expectations of children and young people's behaviour change as they grow up. Behaviour is a universal descriptor, often erroneously used interchangeably with 'problem behaviours'. But for whom is behaviour a 'problem' and to whom is it challenging?

'Problem' behaviours can be both internalising and externalising. Problem situations can be difficult to notice: the young person who finds participation difficult, or who stops eating or starts self-harming. Children who externalise 'problem' behaviour are usually more visible in schools. Resources in schools are often badly skewed towards managing these externalising 'problem' behaviours (Cruddas and Haddock, 2003). It is easy to slip back into a deficit definition of externalising 'problem' behaviours that locates the 'problem' in the child or young person rather than in the social context, in the interaction between people. Transactional analysis, for example, has much to offer in terms of a better understanding of how behavioural transactions position us in particular ways, many of which are unhelpful and unproductive.

A holistic view of behaviour is also closely linked to ecological assessment. Understanding the relations among a person's ecological systems can help us to understand what is going on for them.

Finally, radical and emancipatory theories have a great deal to offer in terms of ensuring that we check our assumptions about what constitutes normative behaviour. As Bayley and Haddock conclude: 'behaviour in schools is a mass phenomenon involving conflicts between different interests, reflecting the hopes and desires of different social classes and national groups' (1999: 28).

Teaching is humanistic

Brendtro and Ness propose that 'Humanistic teaching respects the individuality of each person, thereby seeking to ensure that legitimate adult authority is exercised with consideration of the rights and needs of children' (1983: 21). The difficulty with this tenet is that it obscures the power relations implicit in adult-child relations, although there is some implicit awareness of this in the use of the word 'legitimate'. But who defines legitimacy and under what conditions? Wendy Marshall (1996) points out that 'powerful myths of liberal authority' contribute to the absenting of children's power. The way we categorise 'the child' becomes increasingly confused and contradictory as children get older and become young adults' (cited in Cruddas and Haddock, 2003). Increasingly, the literature starts from the premise that childhood is a socially constructed category.

Crisis is opportunity

Both Egan (2002) and Brendtro and Ness (1987) construct problems as opportunities for growth and development. This is an important shift from a deficit position that considers only crisis, difficulties and risks, to a position that assumes that young people bring strengths and unused potential to the helping process. For Egan, it is 'a question not of what it is going wrong but of what could be better' (2002: 5).

Practice is pragmatic

The pscyhoeducational model draws from a variety of theories and this creates a danger of uncritically engaging with these theories, not all of which are desirable. Brendtro and Ness argue that 'in the final analysis, the most skilful practitioners choose the path that shows most promise' (1987: 24). My concern about pragmaticism is that it is potentially uncritical. Practice is better reviewed as critical, reflective and driven by values. The values that drive learning mentor practice are discussed in chapter seven, and in chapter ten the case is made for peer-based group supervision as a space in which learning mentors can reflect critically on their practice.

This chapter has begun the process of critical engagement with an eclectic model that is historically closely associated with Child and Youth Care practice in North America. The central tenets of the pyschoeducational model, as they are articulated by Brendtro and Ness, are an important starting point in developing some central tenets of learning mentor practice and working towards a model.

As we have seen, the psychoeducational model demonstrates the link between psychology – as the study of human behaviour – and education – as the teaching of human beings. There is no clearly articulated link to the socio-historical context within which this practice is situated, although an awareness of the social aspects of personal development is implicit in much of the way Brendtro and Ness develop their psychoeducational model. What the psychoeducational model arguably lacks, then, is a theoretical link between the social and the personal or developmental-psychological perspectives, as they pertain to education. This is often conceptualised as the tension between development or stage theories in psychology, notably Piaget's work, and socio-historical theories, notably Vygotsky's work.

Following Matusov, I move beyond this perceived tension, arguing that the psychological and social elements of a child or young person's development are mutually constitutive and inseparable (Matusov, cited in Daniels, 2001: 40). Relations between personal and social are re-conceptualised as what Biddell calls a dialectical metaphor of participation (cited in Daniels, 2001: 37). In the participation model, skills are embedded in social activities and meaning is constantly interpreted and renegotiated; the child or young person constantly shapes the process of their development creatively and contributes to defining the direction of their development; and the success of interventions to enhance development is measured by the processes of change of and in participation (Matusov, cited in Daniels, 2001: 40).

This cursory analysis cannot do justice to the complexity of the theories referred to in this chapter. Looking at these models, however, shows that learning mentoring in England can learn from the theoretical anchors of established professional groups in other countries. Much more work must be done in this area if learning mentoring is to deliver on policy developments from a strong theoretical base and if it is to avoid the pitfalls of neo-liberalism.

7

Towards a model of learning mentoring

Although there are, as we have seen, a range of theories that inform learning mentor practice, Egan warns us rightly that 'there must be some integrating framework to give coherence to the entire process; that is, to be effective, eclecticism must be systematic' (2002: 37). Drawing on the traditions of person-centred and positive psychology, Egan's skilled helping model, the basic tenets of the psychoeducational model, Bronfenbrenner's ecological systems theory and the traditions of democracy and education, and social development theory, I offer some basic tenets in a working model of learning mentoring.

Tenet one: The working alliance is primary in the facilitation of learning and participation

The psychoeducational approach, discussed in the last chapter, positions the relationship as primary. Of more use is the notion of 'working alliance' that brings together the best of the arguments for relationship-in-itself, relationship-as-means and solution-focused approaches (Egan, 2002: 43). Egan explores the collaborative nature of helping, the relationship as a forum for re-learning and relationship flexibility (2002: 43-33).

Egan's focus on the collaborative nature of helping connects his work to theories of learning as social practice. 'Helping is not something that helpers do to clients; rather it is a process that helpers and clients work through together' (Egan, 2002: 43). Egan views the collaborative relationship as the vehicle for learning and re-learning. Importantly, he states that 'different clients have different needs, and those needs are best met through different kinds of relationships and different modulations within the same relationship' (2002: 44). Thus Egan is sensitive to how the quality of the relationship affects learning, or to use Rogers and Freiberg's terms, how the interpersonal relationship facilitates learning (1994: 151).

Learning mentors do not only work in dyadic relationships, however. They also facilitate 'working alliances' among groups of children and young people. The case studies in this book explore different forms and structures of participation, through different kinds of working alliances.

Tenet two: Practice is person-centred, value-driven and reflective

We need a person-centred model of practice as identified by Rogers and Freiberg (1994). Learning mentors help children and young people move in the direction of fulfilling their potential. They do this through the relationships or working alliances they establish with them. Egan notes that, as drivers of behaviour in the working alliance, values are 'a set of practical criteria for making decisions' (2002: 45) and that 'helpers without a sense of working values are adrift' (2002: 46). Thus learning mentoring has to be underpinned by a set of clearly articulated values.

A *Value Base* to support the *National Occupational Standards for Learning Development and Support Services* was published in December 2003. This drew on the United Nations Convention of the Rights of the Child and Human Rights legislation:

Practitioners must recognise that the welfare of the children and young people with whom they work is paramount. They must recognise the individuality of each child/ young person and promote their learning, development and welfare. This must be reflected in all work with children and young people and their families/carers. The appropriate legislation framework must be implemented at all times.

Practitioners must adopt a client centred approach based on enhanced inclusion and access, honesty, trust and respect. They will promote equality, respect, diversity and challenge stereotypes, helping to improve the life chances of their clients and the overall effectiveness of service provision. (ENTO, PAULO and TOPSS, 2003b:1)

The values that underpin person-centred practice merit critical analysis. Curiously, the *Value Base* does not set out clearly what these values might be, but merely hints at them in 'honesty, trust and respect'. I particularly want to draw attention to what Egan calls 'values in action' that should guide learning mentor ethical practice and help clarify professional boundaries. Egan (2002: 46) provides a helpful set of four key 'values in action':

- Respect as a foundation value

- Empathy as a primary orientation value

- Genuineness as a professional value

- Empowerment as an outcome value

Each has importance for learning mentor practice.

Respect as a foundation value

As Egan observes, our values generate norms. Respect becomes much more than an attitude or way of viewing others – it is a set of norms. He lists six norms that flow from the foundation value of respect: do no harm; be competent and committed, make it clear that you are for the client; assume the client's good will, do not rush to judgement and keep the client's agenda in focus (2002: 46-47). This set of norms suggests what the *Value Base* might mean by keeping the welfare of the child or young person paramount. This form of respect will help to build trust between learning mentors, the child or young person with whom they are working, and the parents or carers.

Empathy as a primary orientation value

Egan focuses on empathy not as personality trait but rather as an *interpersonal communication skill* (2002: 48). Empathy is a commitment to understanding the young person from their point of view, in the context of their lives and the dissonance between their point of view and reality. In his view, 'empathic helpers respectfully communicate these three kinds of understandings to their clients and generally take an active interest in their concerns' (2002: 49).

To understand people as they are, we must understand both our common humanity and our diversity. Egan argues that helpers need to understand diversity, challenge whatever blind spots they may have and tailor interventions in a diversity-sensitive way (2002: 50-51). He points out an interesting double-bind in working with individuals: the more we understand the broad characteristics, needs and behaviours of the diverse groups with whom we work, the better positioned we are to adapt our interventions to the individual. But conversely, children are individuals, not cultures or sub-cultures of groups. 'Remember, category understanding can destroy understanding as well as facilitate it' (Egan, 2002: 51).

Although it fails to make this explicit, the *Value Base* does go some way towards recognising individuality, while also respecting diversity and challenging stereotypes. Learning mentors challenge stereotyping not just in their practice with individual pupils, but also by monitoring their caseloads in light of equal opportunity, checking whether certain groups of children and young people are over-represented in relation to the school population. If so, the question arises whether this is because the school is targeting a particular group who are underachieving, or whether stereotyping is informing referrals into the learning mentor programme. Learning mentors may well have to challenge institutional blind spots.

Genuineness as a professional value

Egan argues that genuineness, like respect, refers both to a set of attitudes and a set of behaviours (2002: 53). He provides a set of norms: do not overemphasise the helping role; be spontaneous; avoid defensiveness and be open (2002: 53-54). Rogers and Freiberg put this another way. For them, 'realness' is the primary quality that facilitates learning. 'When the facilitator is a real person, being what she is, entering into a relationship with the learner without presenting a front or a façade, she is much more likely to be effective' (Rogers and Freiberg, 1994: 153).

However, a key issue in person-centred practice facilitated in and through the working alliance is knowing and establishing professional boundaries. Learning mentors without boundaries cannot separate themselves from those with whom they work. A lack of professional boundaries leads to practice that is unsafe for both the learning mentor and the pupil. The construction of the professional relationship as a working alliance in the facilitation of learning, begins to clarify where the boundaries might be. But ultimately, as Fewster points out,

> There is no simple formula for establishing boundaries, although it is crucial for all concerned that they be identified and communicated... Although they will vary across individuals and situations, boundaries should be clearly communicated and maintained, once established. If they change over the course of time, this must also be communicated through a process of renegotiation. Above all, it should be remembered that the learning, for both child and practitioner is contained within the process, not in the location of the boundaries themselves. (Fewster, 2002: 14)

Boundaries help to maintain the genuineness or the realness of the working alliance.

Client empowerment as an outcome value

Egan (2002) is clear that the outcome of helping interventions must be empowerment. The opposite of empowerment is dependence, deference and oppression. Colley (2003: 166) puts forward a sobering list of potential outcomes in mentoring programmes which cater to institutional instead of person-centred goals: young people's own needs are ignored and they are pathologised, they experience alienation and deflection away from academic aspirations and they are re-excluded, or their exclusion re-confirmed. This is the opposite of the outcome declared in the *Value Base*: to improve the life chances of children and young people.

At times, learning mentors have to negotiate institutional goals. The case studies that follow reveal how learning mentors employ norms in their practice that generate empowerment and self-responsibility and how they engage pupils in values clarification exercises. While acknowledging that learning mentors and the young people with whom they work will be subject to institutional norms, values and goals, the locus of decisions about goals and targets must remain within the working alliance. And the learning mentors' attitudes and behaviours – their 'values in action' – should always enable empowerment outcomes for the pupils and their families.

What then are the norms of a social-influence process that generate empowerment and self-responsibility and improve the life chances of children and young people? Egan identifies these:

- Start with the premise that clients can change if they choose

- Do not see clients as victims

- Share the helping process with clients

- Help clients see one-to-one sessions as work sessions [or learning sessions]

- Become a consultant to clients

- Accept helping as a natural, two-way process

- Focus on learning instead of helping

- Do not see clients as overly fragile (2002: 56-58)

Empowerment values inhere not just in learning mentoring relationships but also in institutions. Learning mentors and their line managers will need to consider the underlying institutional purposes for which learning mentoring is being used. Power relationships inhere in the relationships among all the individuals involved, from pupils to senior leaders in schools. If learning mentoring is a resource that promotes learning and participation and enables a sense of belonging, independence and mastery in young people, the chances are that the institutional 'values in action' are sound.

I cannot hope to address the complex issues of values, diversity, professional boundaries and the functioning of power in a few pages. I seek only to begin a dialogue about the importance of values, in the hope that it will engender productive debate and critical engagement. There is still much work to be done in this area.

While values are fundamental drivers of professional behaviour, what Colley (2003) refers to as the 'atomising' effects of individual practice can result in practitioners losing sight of values. An essential part of person-centred practice is keeping the person at the centre of practice. Engaging critically in reflective practice is therefore crucial to keeping our values in focus and avoiding formulaic ways of working. Pietroni (1995: 43) argues that critical reflection on practice maximises 'the capacity for critical thought and produces a sense of professional freedom and a connection with rather than distance from clients' (cited in Colley, 2003: 172). Chapter ten of this book presents peer-based group supervision models that provide opportunities for learning mentors to engage in critical reflective practice.

Tenet three: Problems and problem situations are viewed as opportunities

Both Egan (2002) with his model of skilled helping, and Brendtro and Ness (1983) with the psychoeducational model, propose that problem situations present opportunities. Problem situations are defined by Egan as arising 'in our interactions with ourselves, with others and with the social settings, organisations and institutions of life' (2002: 4). Problem solving is an opportunity for learning, but Egan also stresses the need to balance a focus on problem-management with opportunity development. Thus a crisis or problem situation creates two kinds of opportunities: the opportunity to learn how to manage problems better and the opportunity to explore unused potential and personal resources.

If learning mentors focus only on difficulties, problems and problem management, they may soon experience a sense of hopelessness and defeat – and this can only serve to reinforce the hopelessness and defeat some children experience. Brokering opportunities focuses on what can be better. The journey from problem management to opportunity development is one of personal growth, in which the young person's potential is developed. This journey moves away from the language of difficulties, needs and risks towards strengths, resources and resilience. It assumes the agency or active involvement of young people in their own personal growth and the self-recognition of their potential.

Tenet four: Learning is a social process

The model of learning that learning mentors support is not a narrowly prescribed set of outcomes but rather what Vygotsky defined as the space between actual development and potential development. Further, this 'space' is social and participative. Through their working alliances with children and young people, learning mentors make the most of this space. They broker learning and participation opportunities for them, so influencing their cognitive development and strengthening their sense of themselves as learners. Through collaborative activity, they support the development of what Daniels (2001) calls the 'tools for promoting reflection as well as other forms of development.' The case for a transitive model of learning in which participants learn from each other is a strong one.

When arguing for a better understanding of learning as social practice, I positioned this within competing constructions, or learning discourses. What makes learning mentoring different from other mentoring programmes is that learning mentors are *learning discourse guides.* The next case studies demonstrate how learning mentors, as experienced members of the learning community, guide children and young people in a process that involves skilled helping in the social contexts of learning.

In a Vygotskian sense and following Mercer's research into how participation may be supported in the classroom, they use question and answer techniques to guide the development of understanding, they support children and young people in developing ways of solving problems and making sense of experiences and they treat learning as a social, communicative process (cited in Daniels, 2001:123).

Tenet five: The goal of learning mentoring is empowerment and the continued capacity for growth

Empowerment is an outcome value and I have identified the social-influence process that generates empowerment and self-responsibility. But it is not just self-responsibility that is the end goal of learning mentoring. More important may well be the continued capacity for growth.

Dewey maintains that 'the reward of learning is continued capacity for growth' (1916: 82) and that 'the criterion for the value of school education is the extent to which it creates a desire for continued growth and supplies means for making the desire effective' (1916: 44). Rogers and Freiberg ask an important question: 'If education were as completely successful as we could wish it to be in promoting personal growth and development, what sort of person would emerge?' (1994: 314). Their answer: the fully functioning person.

Under what conditions will children and young people have the capacity to grow? Brendtro, Brokenleg and Van Bockern (1990) maintain that children need a sense of belonging in order to be secure in themselves, be able to learn and hence to grow. If a person's sense of belonging is secure, they can develop empathic relationships – what Brendtro *et al* call 'generosity' – have a well-developed sense of mastery and see themselves as competent learners with a strong sense of independence. Brendtro *et al* interpret this as feeling in control and accepting responsibility for themselves and their actions. They represent the four qualities of belonging, generosity, independence and mastery as the four spokes in a wheel they call 'the circle of courage'. For the wheel or circle to be strong and true, all four spokes must be secure. They propose that schools should be 'reclaiming environments' that foster a sense of belonging and help pupils to achieve and develop their sense of mastery by providing opportunities for promoting generosity and generating belonging so that they will have the continued capacity for growth.

Rogers and Freiberg refer to the paradox of personal growth. Under what conditions will children and young people have the capacity to continue to grow?

> All personal growth is marked by a certain degree of disorganisation followed by reorganisation. The pain of new understandings, of acceptance of new facets of oneself; the feeling of uncertainty, vacillation, and even turmoil within oneself are all an integral part of the pleasure and satisfaction of being more of oneself, more fully oneself, more fully functioning. (1994: 323)

Working within this paradox is difficult in institutional settings, particularly those that expect to see positive outcomes of learning mentors' work almost immediately. The expectation among staff in schools that pupils will at once start to learn more effectively can be difficult to manage. The learning mentor, besieged by the frustrations of others when the pupil's personal growth is marked by periods of disorganisation, may be made to feel she has failed. These feelings of failure can create pressures to 'do things differently' that actually move her away from person-centred practice, towards imposing institutional goals on pupils in ways they experience as diminishing and destructive. When this happens, the working alliance is unbalanced and no learning can take place. It is important that learning mentors and those who manage them in schools have strategies for recognising when this is happening, for maintaining person-centred practice and keeping the goal of personal growth firmly in view.

Tenet six: Equality and democracy are integral to the learning mentoring process

In our redefined concept of school improvement (see chapter three), which addresses inequality related to the gaps between achievement and engagement of children from families in different socio-economic positions, learning mentors are an important resource in closing these gaps. Their work is thus crucially linked to the social justice issues of equality and diversity and is part of a democratic tradition in education, which links it with public life. Dewey advocates that 'school facilities must be secured of such amplitude and efficiency as will in fact and not simply in name discount the effects of economic inequalities, and secure to all the wards of the nation equality of equipment for their future careers' (1916: 80).

Dewey identifies two elements which contribute to the democratic ideal in education:

> The first signifies not only more numerous and more varied points of shared common interest but greater reliance upon the recognition of mutual interests as a factor in social control. The second means not only freer interaction between social groups... but change in social habit – its continuous readjustment through meeting the new situations produced by varied intercourse. (1916: 71)

Learning mentors create opportunities for more ways in which common interests among children and young people can be established and shared. They work to create a greater diversity of personal capacities among pupils. Thus have learning mentors changed the social environment of schools – in small but certainly significant ways. Placing learning mentors in schools can and does make schools better places for more children. A significant feature of Dewey's proposition is that schools as institutions can and will adjust to constructive new practices and situations, hopefully becoming more equable environments.

How then to ensure that equality and democracy are truly integral to the learning mentoring process? Or, as Rogers and Freiberg would have it, what are the ways of building freedom to learn? The tenet dealing with values informing practice identifies the values and attitudes that create a facilitative climate for learning. The diagram opposite illustrates how learning mentors facilitate the freedom to learn, and brings the tenets together into a model of learning mentor practice.

In this model, the direction of learning mentoring is always from difficulty and deficit constructions towards opportunity and growth. While acknowledging that learning mentors receive referrals based on difficulties and the needs of the pupil, this is balanced by recognising and moving towards the strengths and personal resources they bring to the learning mentoring process. While it is important to assess what the barriers to learning and participation might be, the working alliance must help to dismantle these barriers through creating opportunities for the pupils to develop their strengths and unused potential. Learning mentors require information about how the pupil is achieving, but they also need to know about the potential for development. Learning mentors work in Vygotksy's 'zone of proximal development': the space between actual and potential development. Although they can and do help children manage problems and problem situations and seek solutions that make sense for them, they also focus on

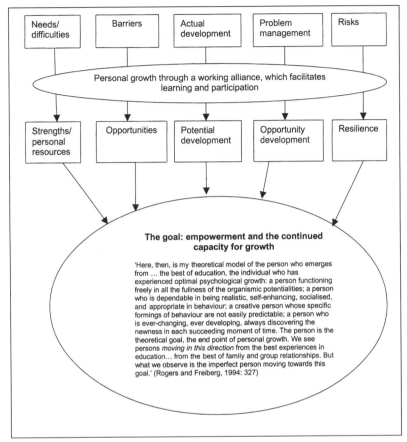

Figure 1: A person-centred, capacity-building model of learning mentoring

developing opportunity. They find ways of promoting resilience through the working alliance. Henderson and Milstein (2003) show that because research into risk does not show cause and effect clearly, it is more effective to build resilience into the environment. The factors they associate with building resilience match our tenets above: providing opportunities for meaningful participation, increasing prosocial bonding, setting clear and consistent boundaries, teaching life skills, providing care and support and setting and communicating high expectations.

Thus the direction of learning mentoring, through the working alliance is always towards personal growth by facilitating learning and participation. The outcome of learning mentoring must be the 'continued capacity for growth' towards what Rogers and Freiberg construct as the fully functioning person and this must include the capacity for creativity:

> This person... could well be one of Abraham Maslow's 'self-actualising people.' With his (sic) sensitive openness to the world, his trust of his own ability to form new relationships with our environment, he would be the type of person from whom creative products and creative living emerge. He would not necessarily be adjusted to his culture and he would almost certainly not be conformist. But at any time in any culture he would live constructively...Such a person would, I believe, be recognised by the student of evolution as the type most likely to adapt and survive under changing environmental conditions. He would be able creatively to make sound adjustments to new as well as old conditions. (1994: 323)

When Robinson *et al* (2001) reported on the importance of creativity and culture in education they made much the same point. The importance of fostering creativity in children and young people is that it meets two related 'challenges' of our society: the personal and the social challenge.

Robinson *et al* define the social challenge as the need to provide forms of education that enable young people to engage positively and confidently with far-reaching processes of social and cultural change (2001: 22). The case studies show how learning mentors' practice supports creativity, curiosity and critical learning.

Another outcome identified by Rogers and Freiberg is that children and young people become constructive and trustworthy (1994: 323). Accordingly, learning mentors build on the trustworthiness of the pupils with whom they work. The case studies demonstrate how learning mentors build on trustworthiness through their working alliances, to enable their pupils to function more fully as constructive and trustworthy beings within their school and communities.

Part of what it means to function more fully is to behave in dependable, though not predictable, ways. This distinction is important. Rogers and Freiberg state that much 'behaviour is a realistic reaction to an accurate apprehension of all [the] internalised evidence' (1994: 324). To re-frame 'problem' or challenging behaviours as realistic reactions is important. What is then needed, through the working alliance, is to create an alternative set of evidence that can be slowly internalised, with the pupil reviewing positive messages about strengths, personal resources, the ability to learn and grow, trustworthiness and so on. They suggest that 'as the individual approaches his optimum functioning, his behaviour, though always lawful and determined, becomes more difficult to predict; and although always dependable and appropriate, more difficult to control' (1994: 325). This is perhaps more significant for schools as institutions than for learning mentor practice: as children and young people move in the direction of growth, their behaviour will be dependable but *more difficult to control.*

This chapter presents a way of thinking about learning mentor practice that anchors practice to theory. Further, it attempts to provide a model of practice that connects it to the broader struggle for forms of schooling that are democratic and equable.

This section of the book has considered theoretical anchors and proposed a provisional model of learning mentoring based on a series of tenets or propositions. The next section tests these tenets by mapping practice in the form of case studies onto an existing set of functions drawn from the *Functional Map for the Provision of Learning Mentor Services.* The functional definition of learning mentoring included in this map has been explored in detail in chapter five. It is broken down into three broad functional areas that make up the key themes of the following three chapters. Chapter eight investigates how learning mentors 'develop and maintain effective and supportive mentoring relationships with children, young people and those engaged with them' (Sauvé Bell: 2003: 1). Chapter nine explores how learning mentoring is a 'complementary service that enhances existing provision in order to support learning, participation and encourage social inclusion' (*ibid*). And chapter ten considers how learning mentors 'work within an extended range of networks and partnerships to broker support and learning opportunities and improve the quality of services to children and young people' (*ibid*).

PART THREE
PRACTICE-BASED EVIDENCE

8

Developing and maintaining supportive mentoring relationships

Colley has called for practice-based evidence (2003: 161). This chapter begins the analysis of learning mentor functions, using illustrative case studies from the practice community. This and the next two chapters examine three broad functional areas, broken down further into detailed functions, to which learning mentor practice is matched. The three broad areas are identified in the *Functional Map for the Provision of Learning Mentor Services* (Sauvé Bell, 2003: 1) as: to develop and maintain effective and supportive mentoring relationships, to provide a complementary service that enhances existing provision and to work within an extended range of networks. A chapter is devoted to each.

First the one-to-one mentoring relationship is examined, showing how ecological assessment and action planning are at the core of learning mentors' work. While learning mentors do offer one-to-one mentoring support in line with more traditional forms of mentoring, they carry out other significant functions. They support attendance, undertake programme development within schools and facilitate access to specialist support services.

As part of developing and maintaining supportive mentoring relationships, learning mentors work to reduce the number of days lost to learning through poor attendance and punctuality, develop programmes to counter early signs of disengagement and contribute to specific interventions to encourage re-engagement. And they refer children and young people to specialist support services.

The one-to-one mentoring relationship

There is much to celebrate in terms of the work of learning mentors in schools, but it is worrying that there is no rigorous model to scaffold the one-to-one mentoring relationship. Many excellent learning mentors in schools have a sound under-standing of the one-to-one relationship and can structure mentoring so that pupils can discover and act on solutions that make sense for them and help them to engage as learners. But a model that helps to make sense of, and make explicit, how skilled learning mentors actually do this is sorely needed.

Egan's pioneering work (2002) offers a generic model of skilled helping that can usefully be applied to many helping profes-sions and I apply it here specifically to learning mentoring. So where Egan refers to 'clients', I take the liberty of referring in-stead to children and young people. I place greater emphasis on learning in personal growth. The outcomes framework in *Every Child Matters: Change for Children* (DfES: 2004e) states that judgements will be made on how schools make provision to support children and young people in developing personally and academically. Learning mentoring, with its focus on per-sonal growth and development through a working alliance, which facilitates learning and participation, is one way that schools can do this.

Egan's model is a 'problem-management and opportunity development' approach to helping. Many pupils are referred into the learning mentor programme because there is a per-ceived 'problem' or problem situation they cannot cope with. Egan defines problem situations as arising 'in our interactions with ourselves, with others and with the social settings, organisations and institutions of life' (Egan, 2002: 4). He stresses that the goal of helping is not to solve problems, but rather to 'help the troubled person manage them more effectively or even transcend them by taking advantage of new possibilities in life' (Egan, 2002: 5). He cites Jones, Rasmuseen and Moffit (1997) who see problem solving as an opportunity for *learning*. They argue that 'engaged learning' can take place in the helper-child relationship.

Egan's model does not focus only on problems and problem situations. He advocates a 'positive psychology' of helping. Because all young people have unrecognised resources and potential, learning mentoring is not only about what is going wrong, but as much about helping pupils recognise the resources they have but are not using or the opportunities they are not pursuing. Egan cites Seligman and Csikszentmihalyi (2000) who called for a better balance of perspectives in the helping professions.

> In their minds, too much attention if focused on pathology and too little on positive psychology: 'Our message is to remind our field that psychology is not just the study of pathology, weakness and damage; it is also the study of strength and virtue. Treatment is not just fixing what is broken; it is nurturing what is best.' (Egan, 2002: 6)

Learning mentoring is not just about fixing problems and problem situations in the one-to-one context; it is also about recognising the strengths, skills, knowledge, abilities and virtues that all young people, even the most troubled, bring with them. It is about helping each of them to take up opportunities and utilise unused potential. It is nurturing what is best.

Positive psychology focuses on unused potential and missed opportunities. Therefore it operates not in a deficit model, which constructs problems as pathologies inherent in individuals, but rather within a social model that constructs problems as opportunities for change. Egan's skilled-helper model can elucidate the conditions under which one-to-one mentoring works.

Case study 3: Skilled helping at George Mitchell Secondary School

John is a pupil whose grandmother looks after him since his mother died recently. He was referred to the LM programme because he had difficulties in relationships with his peers – he had been excluded from school several times for fighting and appeared to have poor organisational skills and a short attention span. He is unpunctual and has a poor record of engaging with learning.

John's performance on standardised assessment tests revealed much higher non-verbal than verbal skill, indicating that he might be capable of learning and achieving well above his current performance.

The LM worked with John for half-hourly, weekly sessions. Initially, these focused on building a relationship of trust. The LM helped John to tell his story, listening carefully to how little he recognised or understood about his own learning potential. She helped clarify some of the distortions he felt about himself as a learner by using a variety of strategies and resources, such as quizzes, checklists, graphs, cartoons and other visual resources and games, to engage John's good linguistic, logical and visual-spatial skills. She also helped him recognise that he has very good interpersonal skills that he could use to his advantage.

Over time, the LM was able to help John identify the right problems to work on. She helped him to understand which problems he could tackle. She worked with John on choosing realistic goals and together they set targets in the areas of planning, organisation, study skills, in-class behaviour, academic learning and developing self-confidence.

Gradually, it became clearer to John that he could learn and he began to develop a good cognitive grasp of subject matter and a better understanding of what was needed to achieve his target grades. But his still underdeveloped organisational skills slowed his progress, as demonstrated by his results in

---

the Autumn term of his final year at secondary school: three C-grades, one D-grade, one E-grade, two F-grades and one U (ungraded). There was a big discrepancy between the grades he obtained and his predicted grades: four C-grades, four D-grades and one E-grade.

The LM and John met regularly between the mock examinations and the final GCSE examinations. The sessions focused on motivation and positive thinking. She helped John with revision planning and timetabling, working to deadlines, mind-mapping and other study skills.

The LM helped John set up a system with a friend so they could revise together and devise quizzes to test each other's memory. She also negotiated with John and a teacher that he receive additional academic mentoring from the teacher.

John's actual results in the Summer term were: one B-grade, six C-grades, three E-grades and one G-grade – significantly better than his predicted grades. John feels that the input from the LM helped him to clarify and prioritise issues and tasks, to focus more quickly and for longer, and to see himself in a more positive light. This progress is clearly reflected in his GCSE results.

Egan's model of skilled helping is set out in three related stages, each framed as a question.

What's going on?

The first stage is entitled 'What's going on?' In this stage, learning mentors help the young person to clarify the key issues. This stage is broken down into three steps: helping the young person to 'tell their *stories*' (Egan, 2002: 27), helping them to 'break through *blind spots* that prevent them from seeing themselves, their problem situations and their unexplored opportunities as they really are' (*ibid*), and then helping them to 'choose the *right* problems and opportunities to work on' (*ibid*, original italics).

In John's case, the learning mentor created a safe space and a relationship of trust in which he felt able to tell his story. Through their conversations, she helped John review what was happening for him both at school and at home. Her overall goal was to challenge and motivate him to manage his learning and his interpersonal relationships more effectively.

The learning mentor realised that John was more able than he thought he was. She helped him to break through the blind spot preventing him from seeing himself as an able and effective learner and helped him move away from his distorted view of himself as a learner. She used quizzes, checklists, graphs, cartoons and other visual resources and games. These strategies enabled him to see himself has having particular learning strengths related to linguistic, logical and visual-spatial skills. Importantly, the learning mentor did not focus only on the problems and problem situations outlined during the referral process. She also focused on and revealed John's strengths and skills and helped him to see these as *opportunities.*

The learning mentor realised that for John to employ these skills to improve his learning, she had to help him to identify issues that would make a difference to his learning. Through his work with her, he realised that he needed to alter his planning and organisation and improve his study skills and in-class behaviour.

What solutions make sense for me?

The second of Egan's stages is to help young people determine outcomes. This stage, too, is divided into three steps: helping young people 'use their imaginations to spell out *possibilities for a better future*' (Egan, 2002: 28), helping them 'choose *realistic and challenging goals* that are real solutions to the key problems and unexplored opportunities identified in Stage 1' (Egan: 2002: 29), and exploring 'the *incentives* that will help them *commit* themselves to their change agendas' (*ibid*, original italics).

Once John's distorted view of himself as a learner changed, he realised that he wanted to achieve academically. He wanted a better future for himself. He made good progress with cognitive understanding of his subjects, but his results were still below both his and his teachers' expectations. The learning mentor helped John to set realistic and challenging goals related to revision planning, timetabling and working to deadlines. These were real solutions to the key barriers to his learning. The learning mentor also explored with him the incentives that would help him commit to his revision planning and keep to deadlines.

What do I have to do to get what I need or want?

The final stage of Egan's model is to help young people implement their plans. Like the previous two, this stage has three smaller steps. The first considers all the possible ways a young person might get what they want and need – action strategies; the second step considers which strategies are best for the young person – best-fit strategies; and the third step is helping young people make plans (Egan, 2002: 30-31).

The case study shows how the learning mentor helped John consider how he might improve his organisational skills. Together, they decided on two action strategies that best fit his circumstances: he committed to revising with a friend and also to working with a teacher who gave him academic mentoring. The learning mentor and John agreed an action plan that helped him to make it all happen. And indeed, it did all happen for John, and he achieved better than his predicted grades.

Egan's skilled helping model makes the one-to-one mentoring process explicit. It is useful in that it focuses not just on problems and problem situations but also on opportunities, development and personal growth. Within this framework, ways of working are agreed, trust is built and roles, expectations and mutual responsibilities are identified. Motivation and challenge are built into the stages of the model. Perhaps most importantly, the aim of the model is to empower young people to improve their learning.

Significantly, learning mentoring as a model of helping is about 'results, outcomes, accomplishments and impact' (Egan, 2002:

7). It is closely linked with the body of theory known as 'solution-focused' therapies. Egan's model is certainly solution-focused in the broader sense. It has a similar philosophical underpinning in that it focuses on resources rather than deficits, possibilities for a better future and helping young people define their own goals and implement a change-plan. It is not necessarily, however, a 'brief therapy'. Egan cites Asay and Lambert's conclusions about the categories of 'clients' who do not necessarily benefit from brief therapy: the poorly motivated or hostile; those with a history of poor relationships and those who expect to be passive recipients of a process (Egan, 2002: 249). All learning mentor programmes are bound to include young people who fall into these categories. The ability of the learning mentor to motivate poorly motivated pupils, form a collaborative working alliance with those who have a history of poor relationships, and help pupils who expect to be passive recipient find a sense of agency, will be crucial. And for these young people, one-to-one interventions may well last for twenty-five sessions or more (Egan, 2002: 249).

Egan believes that his model can best be understood as a 'browser', to borrow a term from the internet. It is a generic model of helping within which learning mentors can choose one specific school or approach or borrow methods and techniques from a range of approaches. It is thus an 'integrating framework to give coherence to the entire process' (Egan, 2002: 37).

Ecological, person-centred assessment leading to action planning

One of the core learning mentor functions, as described in the *Functional Map*, is action planning with pupils. Action planning is not an instrumentalist or mechanistic way of working that reproduces institutional goals or, worse, institutional rules. In Egan's terms, it is about helping children and young people organise the actions they need to take to get results that are meaningful to them. The lack of a plan, 'that is, a clear step-by-step process to accomplish a goal', will keep a young person 'mired' in problem situations (Egan, 2002: 335). So we need to distinguish between informal 'little plans' and formal action plans. Little plans and small action steps are formulated throughout the learning mentor process; whereas 'formal planning usually focuses on the sequence of 'big steps'' (*ibid*). Egan lists the advantages of formal planning, including helping young people to develop the discipline they need, keeping them from being overwhelmed and helping them search for useful ways of accomplishing goals (2002: 336-337). The role of the learning mentor is to help the pupil *shape their plan*, in the context of the working alliance.

Helping a pupil to shape a plan is going to mean different kinds of actions with different children, depending on their age, the nature of the problem situation, the strengths and resources they bring to the process. Action planning is not necessarily done right away in the working alliance. In Egan's model, crafting a plan comes towards the end of the last of his three stages. But Egan talks about building 'a planning mentality into the helping process from the start' (2002: 341).

> Helpers need to see clients as self-healing agents capable of changing their lives, not just as individuals mired in problem-situations. Even while listening to a client's story, the helper needs to begin thinking about how the situation can be remedied and through probes find out what approaches to change the client is thinking about – no matter how tentative these ideas may be... helping clients act in the real world at the start of the helping process helps them develop some kind of initial planning mentality. If helping is to be solution-focused, thinking about strategies and plans must be introduced early. (Egan, 2002: 341)

Learning mentors as skilled helpers and those with whom they work should decide together when and how to produce a plan. Action planning cannot happen at the dictate of the school. For very young children, it is best that little plans or action steps are recorded by the learning mentor. For older children, more formal planning may be appropriate, in which the intention is always to transfer ownership of action planning to the pupil, through the working alliance.

To help a pupil shape their plan, the learning mentor needs to understand their strengths and personal resources as well as the barriers to their learning and participation. There has to be some assessment that underpins the plan. It is useful to conceptualise and contextualise pupils' development within the ecological environment and social contexts of development (see chapter four). If we accept that development and psychological growth are profoundly affected by the broader context and that, as Vygotsky asserts, learning originates in the relationships between people, we have to understand pupils' social environments. How can the environment, as the *medium* in which learning happens, be reshaped and reformed by the pupil's action in it? And what would be the principles of assessment?

The government is developing a Common Assessment Framework aiming to integrate current methods of assessment into one coherent framework. The basic principles which will underpin the framework are that it should be centred upon the child or young person and the whole spectrum of their potential needs; that it is geared towards the delivery of practical and appropriate solutions to their unmet needs, that it should reduce bureaucracy and that it should involve the young people and their families (DfES, 2004a: 39). Though a Common Assessment Framework is welcome, these principles still operate within a deficit model which focuses on needs rather than strengths and resources. Neither are the principles cast within an equalities framework – equal opportunity is not even clearly articulated as a principle. Assessment is an event rather than an on-going process which is person-centred, rooted in development and social environments and collaboratively constructed. The framework assumes that assessment is something that professionals *do to* children and their families.

In the new legislative and policy context, learning mentors are among the professionals who might be involved in common assessment practices. But the assessment practised by learning mentors in their working alliances with pupils is ecological and person-centred. Assessment of this kind interprets the environment as the medium which can be reshaped and reformed in the journey towards personal growth, and not as a fixed 'package of independent variables' (Cole, 1994: 84, cited in Daniels, 2001: 19).

How do learning mentors access information about 'context in action' (*ibid*)? Case study 4 sets out how one London Borough has developed a way of linking assessment to action planning.

Case study 4: Ecological and person-centred assessment in the London borough of Islington

The strand co-ordinator in Islington has worked with an educational psychologist to develop a model of ecological and person-centred assessment that is widely used by LMs in the borough. LMs receive training on undertaking this kind of assessment.

The assessment involves a series of consultation meetings with the pupil's teacher, parents or carers and any other significant adults. The pupil is intimately involved in the assessment process through their working alliance with the LM. The LM then constructs a map of the ecological environments and their impact on learning and participation. The extent to which the map is explicitly constructed with the young person depends on their age, the nature of the working alliance and the strengths and personal resources they bring to the process.

The LM and the pupil will then have a tentative hypothesis, or perhaps several, each of which is tested. For example, if a LM believes a young person has low self-esteem, how have they arrived at this conclusion? Is there any evidence that supports it? This kind of hypothesis testing helps LMs to spot their own blind spots and also to challenge the pupil's blind spots.

Once the hypothesis has been tested, the LM and the pupil can work towards action planning.

This case study shows how the consultation meetings help the learning mentor to build a rich picture of the 'context in action'. The picture or map helps the learning mentor understand the pupil's problems and opportunities in the larger context of their lives. It also helps the learning mentor to keep in Egan's words (2002: 161) an 'evaluative eye' on the working alliance.

The case study also shows that hypothesis testing helps learning mentors see blind spots defined by Egan as being unaware, deceiving ourselves, not wanting to know, ignoring, not caring, not fully knowing or fully understanding (2002: 179). The blind spot may be in the assumption made by the learning mentor about what is going on for the pupil, in which case hypothesis testing is a way of reflecting on incorrect and possibly harmful assumptions. Or it may be in the stories the pupil brings to the working alliance, in which case, the learning mentor's understanding about the context in action can form the basis of a constructive challenge.

However, simply challenging blind spots is not enough. Egan says that we do young people

> ... a disservice if all that we do is help them to identify and explore self-limiting blind spots. The positive-psychology part of challenging is helping clients transform their blind spots into new perspectives and helping them translate these new perspectives into more constructive patterns of both internal and external behaviour. (Egan: 2002: 181)

Context in action can help learning mentors to help pupils to develop new perspectives. In John's case study the learning mentor challenged his distorted view of himself as a learner. She did so on the basis of the evidence she had about his performance on standardised tests. She could then help him develop a new perspective on himself as a confident and able learner, and this resulted in the shaping of a plan that helped John to do very well in his GCSEs.

Case study 5 has been prepared by a learning mentor who uses the Islington model of ecological and person-centred assessment.

Case study 5: Ecological and person-centred assessment practice at Newington Green Primary

The LM at Newington Green Primary School received a referral about James, a boy in Year 4 whose participation and behaviour at school was perceived as a problem. The LM knew that he had attended three primary schools before coming to Newington Green. She wanted to build a good picture of the problems and opportunities in the child's ecological environments. So she consulted with James' teacher and mother. She observed him in the playground and in the classroom and she talked to the educational psychologist about his assessment of the child.

Historically, the family's relationship with the school had been poor. However, the conditions of respectful dialogue that the LM created in the consultation meeting with the child's mother and partner enabled her to obtain valuable contextual information about James' family and community contexts and his social relationships. This helped her make sense in a non-judgemental way of why his attendance was poor, and to think wisely about ways to work with him and his family to improve it.

Through her working alliance with James, the LM created opportunities for him to consider any good reasons for coming to school. They created an attendance and punctuality leaflet together, in which he set out these good reasons. When he was ready to take small action steps, the LM gave him a record book, in which he monitored his own attendance and punctuality. She also created an opportunity for him to be given responsibilities in the morning. The LM continued to meet regularly with his mother and her partner, helping them to be part of the solution. James' attendance improved from 60 percent to 97 percent. His attitude to learning and his willingness to attempt work in the classroom also improved significantly.

The consultation meetings and the observations formed part of the ecological assessment and helped the learning mentor to form a picture about what was going on for James. The context in action helped her understand some of the complex relationships in his life, that were affecting his learning and participation. The learning mentor used this understanding to help James explore his own feelings and thoughts about coming to school, and finally to take action steps towards improving his attendance and increasing his participation. The opportunity she created for him to have responsibilities each morning helped him to begin viewing himself and school more positively. The learning mentor skilfully used ecological and person-centred assessment to support James' attendance at school

Interventions to increase participation, encourage re-engagement, and promote social inclusion

This section describes the kinds of interventions learning mentors can make to increase participation, enhance learning and encourage engagement at school, including programme development. Specific interventions explored are:

- supporting attendance at school

- managing the risk of exclusion and increasing participation

- dismantling school-based barriers

- supporting the development of positive attitudes towards self and others

- motivational programmes that enhance educational achievement.

Supporting attendance at school

The outcomes framework in *Every Child Matters: Change for Children* (DfES: 2004e) states that judgements will be made on how schools make provision to encourage and enable children and young people to attend and enjoy school. We have seen that learning mentors complement existing practices to enable pupils with poor attendance to enjoy school.

Attendance at school is one of two 'engagement' functions, the other being a sense of belonging. Engagement at school is an important educational outcome in its own right (see the PISA results in chapter three). However, the link between attendance and attainment is also important. The NFER findings clearly indicate a relationship between attendance and attainment (see chapter three). They also caution against an uncritical reading of raw data, noting factors other than authorised and unauthorised absence from school are more strongly associated with poor performance (Morris and Rutt, 2004b: 39), including gender, economic disadvantage, having special educational needs and speaking English as an additional language. Consequently, issues of attendance need to be viewed in the light of broader structural and socio-economic inequalities.

In planning and implementing interventions to develop attendance and punctuality, learning mentors work closely with, and complement the work of education welfare officers. There are key differences between the functions of learning mentors and education welfare officers. Most significant is that education welfare officers have statutory duties regarding monitoring attendance and improving attendance at school. Case study 6 demonstrates how learning mentors and the education welfare officer at one school worked together to support a child's school attendance and participation.

Case study 6: Strategies to support attendance at Davies Lane Primary School

Sarah, a Year 6 girl with a history of unpunctuality and poor attendance, was referred to the LM. The case had already been referred to the school's education welfare officer who was providing support for the family to improve Sarah's attendance as her academic work and participation at school were being seriously affected.

The LM offered her one-to-one mentoring sessions. Together, they reviewed her school attendance records and explored the reasons why she couldn't get to school on time. They also discussed how this was affecting her learning. They explored possibilities for improving her attendance and came up with a a number of strategies. The LM helped Sarah to draw up a simple time management schedule, based on waking-up time, time to leave for school, how long the journey to school takes and getting to school on time. They managed to adjust her morning routine so that she could get to school for the start of the day. To reinforce the schedule, she was invited to join the school's breakfast club. She was given a free breakfast as an incentive to attend.

The LM also kept in close contact with Sarah's parents. She held meetings with them to reinforce the schedule that they had agreed and discussed with the family other ways in which they could support positive change.

Over time, Sarah began to appreciate the advantages of coming to school early. She no longer felt embarrassed or anxious about going to class. She had more time to socialise with her friends in the morning, and this improved her mood, social skills and motivation.

Her teacher noticed an improvement in her performance and participation during lessons. Sarah is now ready to begin work at the same time her classmates and eating breakfast helps her to concentrate.

Sarah's punctuality record speaks for itself. Before the LM's intervention, thirty-nine incidents were recorded of her arriving late for school in one academic year. During the year that she was supported by the LM and education welfare officer, she was late for school only five times.

Much as in the previous case study, the learning mentor helped Sarah to take small action steps. However, one key issue emerges particularly clearly in both. Improving James' attendance and Sarah's punctuality and attendance were arguably more institutional goals, and less their own goals. Egan argues against directive styles of intervention, preferring that young people have ownership of goals and that their needs take precedence. He suggests that helping is a 'social influence process' (2002: 55). But he adds this caution: 'social influence is a form of power, and power too often leads to manipulation and oppression' (*ibid*). Colley too warns that mentoring relationships 'obscure our view of power relations' (2003: 2). Both Egan and Colley say that young people have the right to self-determination. Egan talks about empowerment as an 'outcome value' and explores 'norms for empowerment and self responsibility' (2002: 55). As we have seen, power in the learning mentoring relationship is an important and complex issue. Was Sarah empowered by the outcome of the one-to-one mentoring? Was the outcome consistent with her and her family's values or was the goal of improving punctuality and attendance inflicted on them?

Sarah herself defines the outcome in terms of empowerment: she no longer feels embarrassed about coming to school late and she enjoys more time with her friends. The key to the empowerment of children and young people is exactly what the skilled and experienced learning mentor did: she recognised the resources Sarah and her family brought to the process.

The legislative requirements around attendance at school are indeed encoded in a language of deficit. Punitive and remedial action is taken against families. The learning mentor in this case study uses her social influence not to rebuke, punish or disempower but rather to direct the child's and family's resources towards self-determination, so helping them overcome the unequal structures which threatened Sarah's full participation in school life.

Learning mentors often have to find a way between institutional goals and the personal goals of the pupils with whom they are working. They have to keep in mind that the locus of decisions about specific goals and actions remains within the working alliance. Learning mentoring is about decreasing exclusionary pressures and increasing participation. Skilled learning mentors use their social influence towards self-determination and self-empowerment, not seeking to fix individual 'deficits' but rather to discover the resources pupils and their families bring with them.

Managing the risk of exclusion and increasing participation

Supportive mentoring relationships do not only happen in the context of a dyadic one-to-one mentoring relationship. For many children and young people, increasing participation is achieved through brokering relationships with and through their peers. Thus learning mentors play an important role in the capacity of schools to enable learning through group work. The next case study demonstrates how positive change is initiated in the context of group work.

Case study 7: Growing a sense of responsibility and community at Leytonstone Secondary School

The LM at Leytonstone Secondary School worked with the Head of Year 8 on a programme to manage the risk of exclusion for a group of pupils to increase their participation in school and their sense of responsibility. Twenty-two pupils in Year 8 were invited to participate in the programme. Most of those invited were in danger of school exclusion or of exclusion from their peer group. Concerns ranged over attendance and punctuality, social, emotional, behavioural and learning issues. However, the LM worked hard to ensure diversity within the programme. She was rightly concerned that a group identified on the basis of a single type of need – behaviour that could cause harm to themselves or others – could be modelled, and that these behaviours could become normative in the group.

The aim of the programme was to get to know the pupils better and to gain their trust, respect and develop a professional relationship with them that would enable them to take more responsibility for themselves. The LM set up two groups, each with eleven pupils. The groups negotiated their own rules or normative values. They did values clarification exercises and discussed what was good about school and what was difficult. They also discussed ways forward. The LM used her understanding of group processes and the stages or phases groups pass through, to plan and negotiate group activities. Once each group reached a 'norming' phase, she began to negotiate goals and targets. She also brought in a specialist to co-facilitate one of the sessions on communication and anger management.

The LM negotiated and implemented a system of rewards, as incentives for these pupils to commit to the goals and values the group had decided. She then worked with them on possible actions to achieve their goals. The groups looked at how they could contribute to the environment in and around the school. They played an active role in planting spring bulbs around the school site and photos of their efforts were published in a local newspaper. This exposure gave the pupils pride in their achievements.

The LM discovered that there were still unresolved tensions, however, between pupils and members of staff at the school. She planned with the groups to hold a breakfast club and invite the members of staff so that they could begin to build bridges with the pupils.

Following the success of the groups' contribution to enhancing the local environment, the LM looked at other possible actions that could achieve the groups' goals and values. With the LM, the groups decided on a fund-raising event, which involved taking the pupils out to participate in the wider community. She felt that this also demonstrated the school's growing trust in the pupils' ability to act in a responsible way. The Headteacher took part in this event, and the LM felt that this gave the pupils a very positive and important message. The Headteacher commented that after the event members of the group would greet her in the school corridors in a friendly and respectful way, which indicated their increased confidence and sense of belonging to the school community.

Case study 7 demonstrates the appropriateness of Egan's model for scaffolding supportive mentoring relationships brokered through group work. Again, the learning mentor did not focus only on the problem behaviours; she found and created opportunities for the pupils to develop and demonstrate their strengths and personal resources. She conceptualised group tasks as ways of achieving group goals and values, while creating opportunities to transform the attitudes of staff towards the pupils, and for staff and pupils to build bridges together.

The case study fits with Brendtro, Vanbockern and Brokenleg's Circle of Courage (1990), discussed in chapter seven. The skilled and supportive learning mentor created a sense of belonging among these young people by brokering opportunities for them to extend themselves in generous ways in their communities. She created a locus of common interest in the groups and a greater diversity of personal capacities. The pupils began to experience themselves as people who contribute purposively and meaningfully to society. She helped them establish a connection to the school and community. They experienced the joy of giving and creating not just for themselves but also for others, through enhancing the environment and fundraising in the community. These activities heightened their sense of mastery, helped them to take greater responsibility and so function more independently and resulted in an increased sense of belonging and the capacity for continued growth.

The outcomes framework in *Every Child Matters: Change for Children* (DfES: 2004e) states that children and young people have the right to make a positive contribution and to support the community. This is just one case study, but the wealth of evidence in the practice community shows that learning mentors help schools to become 'reclaiming' and inclusive places. This school ended up a better place for these young people.

Dismantling school-based barriers

It is important to consider how schools as institutions create barriers to learning and participation which have an adverse affect on pupils. Two of these school-based issues are examined: barriers in the playground and bullying. How can learning mentors help to create peaceful and inclusive playgrounds and help prevent bullying?

Case study 8: Playground buddies at Cann Hall Primary School

The LMs' playground project at Cann Hall Primary has been extremely successful. The school had inadequate playground facilities and insufficient equipment for children to play with. Behaviour at lunchtimes was becoming a problem.

The LMs wanted to involve the children themselves in a project to change the playground. A whole-school approach was needed. With the support of the senior leadership team, funding was obtained for a training organisation to work with all staff, including mid-day assistants, to decide on what would most improve the playground. Funding was also used to purchase playground equipment.

Twenty pupils were trained in the use of non-equipment games and became the playground buddies. They work to a rota they have drawn up themselves, to share their time and play with children who are lonely or find it difficult to make friends. The activities are monitored and supervised by the LMs. The Computer Club made leaflets about the games. Teachers supported the project by teaching some of the games to their classes during physical education lessons.

As part of their remit, the training organisation undertook a review of the playground and the senior leadership team is currently working with the LMs to implement the recommendations. A working party made up of representatives from the senior leadership team, the LM team, school council, governing body and mid-day assistants is being set up to take this work still further.

Case study 8 shows how the playground becomes a 'reclaiming' environment. Children are seen as part of the solution – rather than the problem – to the barriers to good behaviour in the playground. The playground buddies generate greater belonging by befriending lonely and socially isolated children. They generously give up their own lunchtimes once a week, although this generosity is not selfless. The buddies' sense of their social mastery and responsibility makes them feel good too.

Case study 9 describes a different but equally successful intervention made by learning mentors to help create a peaceful and inclusive playground.

Case study 9: A peaceful playground at Henry Maynard Infant School

The LMs at Henry Maynard Infant School reflected on how much time they were spending trying to resolve squabbles in the playground. Their playground incident book recorded more incidents each day. They observed the behaviour of children in the playground and noticed that the children didn't know how to play or were bored, so they were getting into arguments. They also noticed that if an adult was leading or participating in an activity, children would participate peaceably. They took their lead from these observations to develop a playground project aimed to increase constructive play.

The LMs raised £250 to purchase new equipment, including a 'CONNECT 4' basketball net, throwing net for beanbags, two goals, beanbags, foam Frisbees, foam footballs, ring-toss set, skipping ropes and chalk. The school's site officer kindly painted a sheet of plywood with blackboard paint. He also bought brackets for a hoopla game, which he erected on a wall. The LMs – as they put it – 'scrounged' around the school and found an old parachute, pens, pencils and hoops.

Support staff in the school had always done playground duty with a teacher, so the LMs took their ideas to them. The LMs' plan was to ask support staff to volunteer to supervise activities. The support staff at Henry Maynard are a large group, with a strong commitment to supporting the school, and they agreed. The LMs consider this to be a big factor in the success of the project.

Activities which are supervised and facilitated by members of the support staff include: football, traditional games, CONNECT 4, parachute play, skipping, dance (including a music area), races, hoops and drawing and colouring. Basket ball, throwing net, blackboard and hoopla are not formally supervised, but three adults who patrol the playground keep a watchful eye.

One way in which the playground was evaluated was through monitoring the playground incidents book. Prior to the project, up to three incidents a day were recorded. After the first half-term of supervised activities, only three incidents were recorded throughout.

Ofsted commented on the playground project, saying that the playground was 'outstanding' – one of the best the team had seen. The 2004 Ofsted report includes a short case study of the playground, which they labelled as an example of outstanding practice:

> All children look forward each day to excellent playtime and lunch-time activities... as a mixture of learning and fun. Skilled ancillary helpers enthusiastically lead and participate in numerous traditional and modern playground games, using knowledge of individual children to make sure that they are fully included. In a friendly, quiet area, one helper informally develops children's speaking, listening and social skills.

> In the games groups, children learn individual and team skills not easily developed within the Key Stage 1 curriculum. The youngest children know a variety of signals for beginning a race, and understand the format and conventions of using a simple running track. In football, they amicably take turns to be strikers and goalkeepers, some skilfully impersonate their favourite footballers' styles, others, with encouragement, doing the best that they can without fear of failure or mockery.

> Children confidently suggest the introduction of new games, and they understand that activities are rotated to suit the seasons of the year and the conditions of the playground. These sessions contribute greatly to children's spiritual, moral, social and cultural development, and are a strength of the school.

Building on their success, the LMs are currently developing a winter playground plan. They are keen to acknowledge that the participation of the support staff and the mid-day assistants has been crucial and that without their support, the playground wouldn't be such an agreeable place.

Both playground interventions demonstrate that learning is a social process. It is therefore logical that playgrounds are viewed as learning environments, intimately connected to more formal classroom experiences of participating and belonging. What is remarkable about both case studies is the powerful element of democratic participation. Dewey regarded learning as the accompaniment of continuous activities or occupations which have a social aim and utilise 'the materials of typical social situations' (Dewey, 1916: 288). Both case studies support Dewey's notion that 'education which develops the power to share effectively in social life is moral' (*ibid*).

Preventing bullying

By law, schools have a duty to prevent bullying in all its forms among children and young people. The DfES published anti-bullying guidance in 2002. Brown (2004) argues that an anti-bullying position is based on a 'find it and punish it' conflict model which does little to change a 'bullying tendency' or the culture and practices of bullying in schools. He argues that punitive responses to bullying are counter-productive and that a non-punitive 'bullying prevention' approach aims to empower all elements in the bullying situation – the bully, the victims of bullying, the colluders and the bystanders (Brown, 2004: 8). This is a long-term approach which aims 'to establish a school/community where the action of bullying is made much more difficult because children and adults have established, and maintained, a sensitive awareness of the problems caused, and willingness to act on the insights gained' (*ibid*). Brown argues for a whole-school approach to bullying based on principles of self-help and inclusive group support, which challenges bystander apathy and is consistent with equal opportunity strategies (Brown, 2004: 9). The following case study tells the story of such an approach. The detailed account makes clear the impressive quality of the learning mentor's work.

Case study 10: Support groups at Sybourn Junior

The LM at Sybourn Junior received a referral from the Head-teacher about Ahmed, a child who was being bullied. After consultation with Ahmed's teacher, the LM learned that his attainment and his engagement in his learning had taken a down turn. She decided to set up a 'support group' (DfES, 2002: 28) for him.

The LM arranged a meeting with Ahmed to find out how he was feeling. She began by explaining that she was aware he was not happy about coming to school and said she hoped she could help him with whatever was troubling him. He confided that he was very unhappy because none of the children in his class were nice to him and they called him names. And sometimes he was bullied physically.

The LM explained to Ahmed that she would like to set up a group of children who could support and care for him while he was in school. She used the analogy of a suit of armour: we all have invisible armour that protects us from the negative parts of our lives – unkind comments, someone making fun of us and all the forms that bullying takes. All these negative aspects of life are like arrows being fired at us; if our armour is not strong or has chinks, then the arrows wound us. Our armour is made up of our sense of self – the messages we have received while growing up, comments and actions made by others that go to form our opinion of ourselves, our self-esteem and level of confidence and ultimately what we believe is true about ourselves. The LM suggested that the support group would be a temporary suit of armour to protect him while he was working on growing his own. She asked him about his own armour and he replied that he didn't think he had any at all.

The LM wanted Ahmed's sessions with her to support and protect him so that in time he would be able to learn where his strengths lie and think about himself differently. This would enable his confidence and self-esteem to grow – he would grow his own suit of armour.

She arranged with Ahmed's class teacher for him to spend a lesson in another class while she spoke to the rest of his class. She told Ahmed what she was going to say and got his approval. She began by clarifying her role in the school and explaining to the class how she sometimes asked children to help her carry out that role. She told them, without naming anyone, about a child who was having a really hard time at the school. She listed all the things that were happening to the child and took time to describe the feelings the child was experiencing. She then asked if anyone in the class had ever felt that way. A good many hands went up – including the main perpetrator's – and the class embarked on a lengthy sharing of such experiences and the feelings that went with them.

This stage of setting up a support group is vital as it is empathy that enables even young children to relate the situation to themselves and see the situation for others as real. With the LM, the class looked at the different roles in a case of bullying: the perpetrators, the encouragers and the bystanders, and how each role helps prop up another. She ended by thanking the class for sharing their feelings and praised their honesty and emotional intelligence. She then asked if there was anyone who felt they could and would be prepared to make a difference to the child she had told them about by working as part of a support group. Almost every hand in the class went up. Only two children didn't put their hands up: one who was heavily involved in the bullying and another who was not. The LM told them that this was about Ahmed and said she would pass on the good news to him and that together they would decide who to invite to join his support group.

The LM informed Ahmed about how things had gone in class and they discussed who they would choose as part of the support group. She explained that they would need to agree all choices. This is important, as it is the first opportunity for him to feel empowered, his first taste of having some control over the situation. After some discussion they settled on nine children, three girls and six boys.

The LM wanted at least one of the main perpetrators to be involved in the group so he could experience 'putting things right' and thus develop his emotional intelligence and build conflict resolution skills. Including a child who has been part of creating the problem is a good strategy as it not only gives that child a new set of guidelines to follow but also sends out a clear message to others that change is not just possible but also desirable and admirable.

The LM then held a meeting with the chosen children and explained why they had been chosen. It is important to give each child a reason for their selection and what it was felt they could bring to the group. She also stressed that it was a huge compliment to them and something to be proud of. The LM explained how the group would work: they looked at the different parts of Ahmed's day and discussed who in the group would be with him at any time. Each child came away with defined areas of responsibility and all agreed to work in pairs. Through discussion they came up with certain scripts and strategies to be used if other children were causing a problem. One of the group collected Ahmed from class to join the meeting; this small gesture was the first step in the change about to take place. The meeting concluded with Ahmed feeling much more positive and when they left the room, one of the boys had his arm around Ahmed's shoulder.

The LM kept in contact with the family throughout the process so as to give and receive feedback on developments.

The LM arranged to meet separately with the two children who had not put up their hands in class. One boy felt he hadn't been part of the problem, while the other said he felt confused as to whether he should put up his hand as he knew he was one of the main causes of the problem. This meeting allowed the LM to let this boy, Mark, know that she cared as much about how he was feeling as she did about Ahmed. They were able to discuss Mark's feelings while he was bullying and how he now felt when he reflected on it. They explored the feelings of self-importance he had experienced while bullying and how he could now recognise these to be what the LM calls 'fake feelings' – because when she asked him to search for those feelings, he realised they had evaporated and had left him feeling empty. But when they compared his other feelings, for example the love and affection he felt for his family or his pride when he received real praise, he realised that those feelings remained constant and accessible when tested. They spent some time looking at where else he could derive feelings of self-importance that would be real, and lasting. The LM reassured him that it is not only 'bad' people who do bad things but sometimes good people as everyone is capable of making mistakes. She believed it was important for Mark to understand that the very fact he felt ashamed meant that he could re-classify himself in his own mind as a good person who had made an error of judgement. So the erstwhile bully experienced growth in his emotional learning and could go on to being a happier and more successful individual in terms of his inter-personal and intra-personal skills.

The LM held weekly support group meetings where successes, obstacles and strategies were shared. It was important for the supporters themselves to receive support from within the group. The group looked at how Ahmed was getting on and where he wanted to be. They drew a chart to show each week's progression. Some weeks there was none because a couple of boys continued to bully him. One of the group described it as being 'like someone's put an obstacle in our way so we can't get to where we want to be'. The LM encouraged the group to discuss how they could overcome this obstacle. One child suggested inviting the perpetrators to their next meeting. This was agreed as the best way forward, as the group felt that if they could explain what they were trying to achieve, the perpetrators would understand how their actions were making it impossible. One of the group remarked that the culprits needed to know that the group did not approve of their actions and were not prepared to let it continue.

The boys were asked to attend a meeting where the group showed them the pathway they were trying to take Ahmed along and how their actions were creating obstacles and preventing progress. They related how Ahmed was feeling and asked direct questions to discover why the boys felt they had a right to go on bullying him. The boys were informed that they would be given another chance to think about how they chose to act and to decide if they were ready to change. The LM took a back seat during the meeting so the real power of peers in school could prevail.

After the boys had left, the group discussed what strategies they would use if the culprits did not mend their ways. The group felt the boys' parents should be informed and sanctions put in place. However, this proved unnecessary as the strategy succeeded and the group were able to continue the journey.

The LM explained that the aim of any support group was for Ahmed to reach a place where he would no longer need it. While charting progress, the LM included small reviews along the way and it was revealing that the group always rated Ahmed's progress as greater than he did. This is indicative of the complex long term psychological effects bullying has. Outwardly the group can see real change, the unkind comments and abuse have stopped and Ahmed appears happier, secure and well cared for. But for Ahmed there is always the possibility that the bullying may begin again and dread lest this be the day that his armour is tested. Until Ahmed's armour is firmly in place, he cannot mentally move to the belief that others have truly changed. Ahmed had been so immersed in self-doubt that it was vital for the LM to understand that it would take time to free him.

The support group kept going for almost sixteen weeks until Ahmed was able to say that, even if the arrows come some days, 'they sort of just fall off and don't hurt anymore.' Towards the end of the sixteen weeks, he said: 'Now I know if someone wants to fire an arrow at me, it's their problem not mine.'

Ahmed has gone on to become a confident child who has come full circle in his journey and is now part of a support group for another bullied child, where his understanding and unwavering support is proving invaluable. His armour has grown.

The learning mentor in this powerful intervention truly establishes a Circle of Courage in the support group, which not only generates a greater sense of belonging in the focus child but creates an opportunity for other children to extend themselves on his behalf. The support group uses empathy as what Egan refers to as a 'primary orientation value' (2002: 48). They make a commitment to understanding Ahmed from his point of view. The children in the group developed the personal capacities and courage to challenge peers who continued to bully. They helped Ahmed build resilience – his 'suit of armour' – thereby helping to empower him. By bringing out the strength and personal resources of the child they are supporting, they discover the best in themselves.

In the next case study, the learning mentors work with the support of the school's senior management team to develop a whole-school approach to preventing bullying.

Case study 11: A strategy to prevent bullying at Barclay Junior School

The LMs at Barclay Junior school led the development of a strategy to identify and prevent bullying. With the headteacher's support, questionnaires were distributed to all the children. Children in the gifted and talented programme analysed the responses and showed the findings as simple bar charts. One finding revealed that bullying was going on in the boys' toilets. To prevent this, pupil monitors were appointed to keep an eye open for actions that might lead to bullying. Other strategies put in place by the LMs in response to the questionnaires were:

- a 'What is Bullying Board' for children to record their views

- working with the personal, social and health education co-ordinator to deliver a unit of work on bullying

- a dedicated quiet space in the school hall where children could go during breaks.

In addition the school progressed its work on bullying through a peer buddy programme, implemented by the LMs. The LMs stress that work to prevent bullying has to be linked to whole-school initiatives, such as making the playground pleasanter, developing a healthy schools programme and informing parents and carers about what is being done to prevent all forms of bullying.

Interventions that develop positive attitudes in pupils

The case studies have described using the pupils as buddies to promote a peaceful and inclusive playground and help prevent bullying. The next show how the resources of pupils can be used to create schools as 'reclaiming' and inclusive environments. Julia Baker, a learning mentor in a Sheffield school, developed innovative and impressive peer-mentoring and peer buddying programmes. She distinguishes between peer mentoring – mostly in secondary schools – where older pupils support young pupils in the traditional role of mentor and guide, and peer buddying which applies children's skills of helping in everyday interaction with peers, most commonly used in primary schools (2003: 32). However, as case study 12 demonstrates, peer mentoring can also be implemented successfully in primary schools.

Baker's work is located in the broader field of peer support as an effective strategy to develop pupils' positive attitudes towards themselves and others. She cites Carr (1994), who identified more than thirty different terms to define peer support systems. Baker provides a useful overview of the main peer support programmes: peer mentoring, peer tutoring, peer education, peer researchers, peer buddies, peer mediation, peer counselling and peer listening (2003: 32). Peer support is a vital but underused resource for school improvement. It is also connected to work in 'pupil voice' and the contributions pupils can make as partners in school improvement, through school councils but also through other innovative programmes. There are many ways in which learning mentors can contribute to peer support and 'pupil voice' programmes but space allow for only one peer mentoring programme to be described here. We see how, by implementing peer mentoring programmes and brokering supportive relationships between peers, learning mentors increase participation. At the same time, they develop supportive and supervisory relationships with the peer mentors.

Case study 12: Peer mentoring at Coppermill Primary School

The LM at Coppermill Primary set up a peer mentoring programme in September 2003. She delivered comprehensive peer mentoring training to sixteen Year 6 pupils, to increase confidence and raise self-esteem by giving pupils some responsibility for younger peers. Pupils who had a wide range of skills and ability were trained, including three pupils who were receiving one-to-one mentoring from the LM.

The peer mentors meet weekly for forty-five minutes and work with their younger 'buddy' in Year 3 or 4. They fill in a weekly report and action plans, supervised by the LM. Each peer mentor has their own folder and buddy book, which they use to report back to the LM and share any concerns.

The peer mentors have taken their responsibilities seriously and work with commitment and enthusiasm. The programme carries prestige among their friends and this has boosted their confidence and their motivation to learn. The younger buddies have enjoyed having the support of an older peer mentor and have made progress in many ways.

One peer mentor whom the LM initially had doubts about including in the training because of his challenging behaviour turned out to be a triumph. As she writes: 'This boy is without doubt the most caring, consistent and dedicated of all my [peer] mentors and his behaviour in class and at playtimes has changed beyond all recognition. He has developed a belief in himself that I have not seen before and a willingness to help younger children in school... As a school we really embrace this programme!'

Among the benefits of peer mentoring and peer buddying outlined by Baker are: promoting and developing a caring school community; contributing to school effectiveness and school improvement; promoting the citizenship agenda; giving the message to the community that relationships are important; reassuring parents and families that children will be safe; and giving the message that inclusion is a priority (Baker, 2003: 2).

Baker also maintains peer mentoring supports academic achievement. If, as Vygotsky argues, all learning happens first at the social level, in the interaction between people it makes sense to find and implement ways for pupils' social relationships to enhance their learning. The relationships between pupils are a vastly under-estimated and under-used resource in school improvement. Peer mentoring programmes successfully begin tapping that resource by including pupils as school improvement partners.

Case study 13: Peer mentors supporting learning at Highams Park Secondary School

The LM at Highams Park School set up an effective peer mentoring programme, based on Baker's training programme. Peer mentoring is advertised, and pupils apply for a place on the programme. They must complete an application form, ask an adult for a reference to support their application and then attend an interview. Those who succeed at interview receive two full days peer mentoring training delivered by the LM. Peer mentors have to record their learning outcomes in a workbook. The programme is accredited by the Open College Network as a level one, two or three certificate in mentoring skills.

Peer mentors support the pastoral work of the school in many ways. Historically, they have had a role in supporting transfer arrangements, giving an introductory sessions to Year 6 children at the school's partner primary schools. Referrals are taken initially from teachers in primary schools and, following transfer to secondary school, the Head of Year 7 refers young people to the peer mentoring programme. Participation in the programme is entirely voluntary.

Peer mentors offer a listening, non-judgemental ear, appropriate advice, information about clubs and after school activities, help with homework, help with personal organisation, help – where appropriate – with sorting out problems, and give encouragement and support. They also offer specific support to younger pupils who are being bullied, who identify themselves through the school's intranet and they provide a drop-in clinic. Pupils from all year groups can email a peer mentor through the intranet, thus widening access to the peer mentor programme.

Peer mentoring is managed and supervised by the LM, who meets regularly with each peer mentor. The LM also ensures that she evaluates the service regularly, by consulting with young people referred into the peer mentoring programme.

More recently, the school has developed its peer mentoring programme to support learning as well as personal development and well-being. Peer mentors have been trained in the use of the *Learning Challenge* materials (DfES: 2003d) as peer 'coaches'. The aim of the *Learning Challenge* is to help pupils improve their organisation of themselves and their learning. There are seven challenges in the *Learning Challenge*, each dealing with a different aspect of personal organisation or the organisation of learning. Pupils who could benefit from additional support in developing the skills for learning are referred to the peer mentors who work through the appropriate learning challenge. Learning within the peer mentoring relationship is perceived as a structured, social activity in which young people develop skills to support their learning. Thus, the peer mentoring programme now contributes to the care and support of the pupil community and also, more directly, to raising attainment.

Case study 13 demonstrates how peer mentors support a transitive and social model of learning, and hence school improvement. By widening areas of shared concern, as Dewey proposes, peer mentors are part of the liberation of a greater diversity of personal capacities.

Motivational programmes that build self-esteem and educational achievement

So far this chapter has explored dyadic one-to-one mentoring relationships, the facilitation of mentoring relationships in groups, and with peers. I turn now to the development of mentoring relationships through motivational programmes, many of which take place in clubs out of school hours. Learning mentors run breakfast clubs, dance, drama, music, sports and art clubs. These have in common a commitment to enhancing motivation and building self-esteem by tapping in to pupils' strengths, intelligences and particular ways of learning.

Case study 14: Building on and sustaining good work – a social club at Whitehall Primary School

The LM at Whitehall Primary School was aware that many of the children were under-confident and experiencing social difficulties. Some had been part of a Pyramid Scheme* the year before. The LM planned an after-school club to sustain the good work of the Pyramid Scheme.

She obtained funding to pay for another member of staff to co-facilitate the club with her. With two members of staff, the club's membership could extend to twelve children.

The LM used the structure of the original Pyramid Club and broke sessions down into four activities:

■ Eating together: all members were encouraged to sit around a table, so affirming this as an important and special time. The LM also used this time to explain the programme of activities for the session.

■ Mini-circle time: the LM used this time for the group to find out more about one another and to encourage members of the group to speak and listen to each other. Some members found it difficult to take turns, or even to speak or listen.

■ Art activity: each week, the group undertook a different art activity – paper maché, sewing, puppet-making, modelling, biscuit decoration and glass painting.

■ Games: members spent the last period of time choosing from a selection of games or play activities, including Lego.

The outcomes of this club have been very positive. Children have developed friendships within the group and their confidence has grown. One girl who refused to speak at all in school now joins in circle-time, talks to her peers and to members of staff and has even begun to initiate conversations herself. Before joining the club, she had a record of poor attendance at school. Following the formation of a friendship at the club, her friend now calls for her in the morning, and her attendance at school has improved.

One boy who joined the club found it difficult to play with other children. Even after joining, he chose to play with Lego on his own for the first few sessions. He now confidently engages in social play with other children.

Many of the children in the club initially found it difficult to play games, finding turn-taking and 'losing' particularly hard. These skills are now developing well.

The club is reviewed every half term by the Headteacher, Special Educational Needs Co-ordinator and the LM.

* *The Pyramid Club was run by the Waltham Forest Pyramid Scheme, which is part of the National Pyramid Trust, a registered charity. It is an organisation that helps primary school children to fulfil their potential by building their self-esteem and resilience. The aim is to recognise and respond positively to children's social and emotional needs, usually through clubs that help children to make friends and build their self-esteem.*

Their work in clubs and out-of-school-hours learning opportunities connects the work of learning mentors to informal and community education programmes. Daniels analyses the social contexts of learning:

> After-school clubs are used as settings in which the richness of the community knowledge funds can be brought together with the academic purposes of teaching. After-school clubs were designed so that multiple goals could be pursued: the children engaged in meaningful activities in which valued outcomes were achieved. (Daniels: 2001: 118)

Learning mentors ensure that learning is facilitated in the context of these activities. Like peer mentoring programmes, after-school clubs are fostering, nurturing, cultivating places that build on the social relationships between children and young people that create the conditions for personal, social and intellectual growth. Clubs can form part of the extended services that schools are now encouraged to offer.

Facilitating access to specialist support services

Learning mentors do not make all interventions themselves. As a consequence of ecological assessment, learning mentors identify appropriate interventions that could be made. Part of developing and maintaining supportive mentoring relationships can be identifying appropriate support services within and outside the school and negotiating their possible role with the individual pupil or group, as illustrated in case study 15.

Case study 15: Stress management and study skills at Walthamstow School for Girls

During the one-to-one mentoring process with several pupils in their final year of secondary school, they and the LM identified that pupils were extremely anxious about the imminent final examinations. They were experiencing symptoms ranging from 'tolerable' feelings of 'being out of control' to more serious, and in some cases debilitating conditions like insomnia, depression and anxiety attacks.

The LM decided to bring in specialist support for these pupils. She approached a sports psychologist to design and facilitate a programme to teach the girls stress-management skills and to facilitate their developing personal resources that would enable them to manage their stress.

One hour sessions were held weekly over six weeks for thirteen Year 11 pupils. The programme was designed as an experiential course and included the theory and practice of anxiety and stress management. The girls were led through stress-relieving exercises each session, such as breathing and relaxation techniques, improving concentration and study/ revision skills. The idea was to introduce self-management skills so they could develop confidence and personal resources in response to stressful situations.

After three sessions, the participants reported improvements in their general physical and emotional well-being. Also that they were benefiting from the time-management and study skills. They were able to plan and pace their coursework and revision timetable thus reducing the potential for anxiety and stress-related symptoms.

In the final evaluation forms the pupils said they had learned:

'How to stay calm while revising and sitting an exam'; 'Breathing techniques to slow my breathing and keep calm'; 'How to revise properly'; 'The four C's: Calmness=concentration=competence=confidence'; 'That by breathing and controlling my emotions, I can bring down my anxiety and stress levels. That understanding myself better, I can perform better.'

The LM observed that the study skills and revision techniques had boosted confidence and with it motivation.

Overall, the effect on the school's attainment profile was impressive. The collective results were fourteen A* grades, twenty-five A-grades, twenty-eight B-grades, twenty-seven C-grades, six D-grades, one E-grade, seven F-grades and one G-grade. All the D-grades were achieved by pupils who also achieved 5 A- to C-grades. Two of the E-grades were achieved by two pupils who also achieved fourteen A to C-grades between them. One of the seven F-grades was achieved by a pupil who also achieved four B and five C-grades. Four of the E and four F-grades were achieved by a pupil who has learning difficulties. She was awarded two school prizes: the learning development prize for effort and the prize for progress and personal development.

In the evaluation forms, many participants recommended that the course should be offered to Year 10 pupils at the beginning of the GCSE course. The LM is taking up this recommendation.

This case study shows a learning mentor listening carefully to the stories of stress and anxiety the pupils related in their one-to-one mentoring sessions. These girls were committed to learning – their problem was managing their personal anxiety and developing the personal resources to organise themselves and study effectively. In thinking with them about solutions that made sense, she created an opportunity to help them significantly. The best-fit strategy here was not an individual but a joint strategy that she brokered. She brought in a specialist, the sports psychologist, to help the girls develop their personal resources for managing anxiety, and also to plan their coursework and revision timetable. The sports psychologist helped them choose realistic goals for meeting their coursework deadlines and for revising. Their regular attendance over the six-week course was an incentive to commit themselves to their change agenda.

Case study 15 demonstrates flexible use of Egan's model. Egan reminds us that 'Helping is for the client. Clients' needs take precedence over any model' (2002: 33). Skilled learning mentors do not engage mechanistically in each stage of the model. As in this case, the steps can be intermingled and learning mentors may find themselves moving backwards and forwards. Egan provides another metaphor for his model:

> A helping model is like a map that informs you, at any given moment, 'where you are' with a client and what kinds of interventions will be most useful. In the map metaphor, the stages and steps of the model are orientation devices. At its best, it is a shared map that helps clients participate more fully in the helping process. They too need to know where they are going. (Egan, 2002: 35)

The learning mentor used the stages and steps flexibly but maintained focus and direction in helping the pupils manage their anxiety and study more effectively. She was clear about her role in the helping process and also the extent of her skills. She was able to facilitate access to a specialist at just the right point, and to agree with him what his roles and responsibilities in the programme would be. She nevertheless maintained oversight of the programme, monitoring and recording its effectiveness.

This chapter has looked particularly at how learning mentors develop and sustain mentoring relationships with children and young people. The next considers how learning mentor provision can complement and enhance existing provision in schools.

9

Learning mentoring:
a complementary service

The managers of learning mentors must integrate learning mentor programmes into school structures (see chapter four) to ensure that they become 'a complementary service that enhances existing provision in order to support learning, participation and encourage social inclusion' (Sauvé Bell, 2003:1). According to the *Functional Map for the Provision of Learning Mentor Services*, this broad functional area breaks down into three 'detailed' functions:

- assisting children and young people to make a successful transfer between educational establishments and transition at key stages in their learning

- contributing to the comprehensive assessment of children and young people entering educational establishments and the review of their progress and achievements

- contributing to the identification of barriers to learning for individual children and young people and providing them with a range of strategies for overcoming the barriers. (Sauvé Bell: 2003)

Managers should take account of the learning mentors' role in transfer and transition arrangements, assessment of new entrants and identification procedures, when they consider how learning mentors can provide a complementary service to enhance existing provision. The rest of this chapter analyses each 'detailed' function and how each is interpreted in practice.

Improving transfer and transition arrangements
Learning mentors' contribution to helping young people manage change and respond to challenges

In 1999, the DfES commissioned research into the effects on pupils' progress and attitudes to learning at key points of change: transfer – the move from one school to another – and transition – the move from one year to another within a school. The research, *The Impact of School Transitions and Transfers on Pupil Progress and Attainment* (Galton *et al*, 1999) demonstrated that two out of every five children fail to make expected progress in the transfer between primary and secondary school. This research is confirmed by the Ofsted 2002 report *Changing Schools: an evaluation of the effectiveness of transfer arrangements at age 11*. Ofsted noted the need for schools to 'do more to prepare pupils for any significant changes in teaching approaches between Key Stage 2 and Key Stage 3 ... [and] evaluate more systematically the impact of transfer arrangements on the progress and attitudes of pupils' (Ofsted, 2002: 2).

The research collected data not only on children's progress but also on their attitudes. It measured their anxiety, motivation and enjoyment. Significantly, pupils 'were more motivated immediately after transfer but motivation then declined during the remainder of the year' (Galton *et al*, 1999: 10). Another feature of the research also deserves attention:

> On the assumption that underachieving pupils find school less attractive and are not motivated to work hard, we might expect strong positive associations between pupils' academic performance, motivation and enjoyment of school. But in the ORACLE replication study, there was a small but significant

correlation between progress and enjoyment at school, indicating that some pupils doing well academically were being
'turned off' school. When this finding is taken along with what
we know about the phenomenon known as the Year 8 dip, there
are grounds for serious concern. These 'middle years' of
schooling may be exerting a disproportionate and negative influence on pupils' achievements and their subsequent subject
and career choices. (Galton *et al*, 1999: 10-11)

This is an important finding. The focus of concern and activity
is usually around transfer between schools, whereas this
research indicates that 'attention need to be directed more
evenly across the whole of the middle years of each phase of
schooling as pupils move from one year to another' (Galton *et
al*, 1999: v). Clearly, attention also needs to be paid to pupils'
engagement, motivation and enjoyment of their learning.

When theorising about the hiatus in progress and what schools
can do when young people become disengaged from their
learning after transferring to secondary school, Galton *et al* cite
Lehelma and Gordon's (1999) work on 'learning to be a professional pupil'. The research demonstrates that while schools
are increasingly good at managing the administrative or
bureaucratic side of transfer and meeting social and personal
needs, curriculum continuity, pedagogic issues and managing
learning are relatively neglected. The National Primary and Key
Stage 3 strategies are apparently attempting to address the issue
of curriculum continuity. But few schools (the research estimates between two and five percent) have joint programmes of
teaching and learning or teacher exchanges between primary
and secondary schools to encourage an understanding of pedagogical differences between the sectors. Even fewer schools (the
research estimates two percent) focus on programmes that support young people in managing their own learning or becoming
a 'professional learner'.

Galton *et al* and the findings from PISA 2000 (see chapter three)
are clear that engagement is an important educational outcome
in its own right. So how can young people can be supported to

engage in and manage their own learning? In an unpublished presentation, Galton states: 'We need young people who can sustain, through their primary and secondary schooling, an enthusiasm for learning, confidence in themselves as learners and a sense of achievement and purpose.'

Galton *et al* describe a professional learner as one who has high motivation and engagement, and enjoys and can manage their own learning and who achieve highly. Professional learners sustain their enthusiasm for learning across critical periods of transfer and transition. They understand the purposes and structures of learning.

The outcomes framework in *Every Child Matters: Change for Children* (DfES: 2004e) states that children and young people have the right to make a positive contribution, and that judgements will be made on how schools make provision to help pupils manage changes and respond to challenges in their lives. How can learning mentors help to keep young people engaged as learners during the period of transfer and how can they re-engage disengaged pupils as professional learners and support them in their personal growth?

Creativity is an important factor. Galton and MacBeath (2002) analyse the effect of the national curriculum on a 'broad and balanced' curriculum offer: music, art and design are squeezed out of the curriculum and there is less time for pursuing young people's interests – what they call 'magic moments'. They point out that the assessment and testing regime has generated high levels of stress among young people and the adults who work with them. They have to cope with more coaching, revision and booster classes, and less informal feedback about their learning.

In this climate, learning mentors have an important role in contributing to a school's capacity to offer creative and cultural opportunities, as a way of keeping young people engaged in their learning and helping them to understand and manage change.

In *All Our Futures: Creativity, Culture and Education,* Robinson *et al* (2001) define creativity as 'imaginative activity fashioned so as to produce outcomes that are both original and of value' (Robinson *et al*, 2001: 29). They propose that 'there are many factors affecting motivation and interest in education. But one of the most effective solutions is to develop active forms of learning which engage the creative energies of young people'. Participating in creative living and being able to adjust creatively to the far-reaching processes of change mean functioning better (see chapter seven). Case study 16 illustrates one way in which learning mentors worked together to keep young people actively and creatively engaged in their learning.

Case study 16: Magic moments – *Condition of the Primary Pupil*

LMs in ten Waltham Forest schools worked with children and young people on a multi-media creative arts project about change and transitions. The project aimed to celebrate children's creativity. Work from this project was exhibited for two weeks at a local art gallery under the title 'Transitions: children's art about change', and also exhibited as part of the local *Imagine 2012* event. LMs hoped to create an opportunity for young people to explore and express their feelings about change. By taking children's art out of the school and into the gallery, the exhibition aimed to affect the children's view of their own work and to change public perception of children's art. Exhibiting the art in a gallery space provided the opportunity for the community and the broader public to engage with and reflect on children's art and their learning. Their comments were recorded in a visitors' book.

A member of the public wrote: 'This has been fantastic. I love the boxes of memories and the string things. The next generation of Brit Artists!'

A girl who contributed to the exhibition and attended the private view with her parents wrote: 'I am one of the artists of today's event, and I am very pleased with the turnout of people who attended.'

A parent of another girl who contributed to the exhibition, wrote: 'I've watched my daughter create this collage from the beginning. I'm very impressed with the results and people's comment and praises [in the visitor's book]. I am very proud of her work and this show.'

A school effectiveness advisor who visited the exhibition wrote: 'An inspiring art collection and excellent collaboration of schools through LMs.'

The process of creating the art was as important as the finished product. It sought to help young people find meaning and make sense of themselves, their changing identities and the changes that transferring to secondary school would inevitably bring. LMs planned to develop active and creative forms of learning so as to sustain motivation and interest in education.

Two LMs from different primary schools who worked together to create a developmental process best reflects these ideas.

Year 6 pupils from Sybourn Junior and Thomas Gamuel Primary School worked on a joint project inspired by the French artist Armand Fernandez Arman, who created 'Condition of Woman Number 1' exhibited at the Tate Modern. The pupils visited the Tate Modern Gallery with LMs and looked carefully at Arman's work. After drawing and discussing the work, the pupils made their own constructions to represent their time at primary school.

Pupils showed remarkable insight into Arman's work. Some of their interpretations are reproduced below:

'The box is glass so that the artist could see through to the next stage of his life – his future. '
'There is no lid so things can't get out – that part of his life is sealed and finished.'
'The broken glass is his sadness – the break-up of his marriage'
'The pedestal is really shiny and pretty. This could describe the happy parts of his relationship.'

One pupil suggested that their contribution to the exhibition be called *Condition of the Primary Pupil*, to reflect what they had learned about Arman's work and their own change processes.

This project created an opportunity for learning mentors and the pupils with whom they worked to begin to engage with two of the major challenges for education identified by Robinson *et al*: the social challenge and the personal challenge. They define personal challenge as the need to develop the unique capacities of all young people and to provide a basis on which they can build lives that are purposeful and fulfilling (Robinson *et al*, 2001: 18-25). *Condition of the Primary Pupil* supported this process by beginning to make sense of personal change – both the change Aman lived through and their own personal changes in terms of transfer to secondary school and the changes imminent in their burgeoning adolescence. By encouraging an active and creative exploration of change, *Condition of the Primary Pupil* helped the children to reflect purposefully about these changes. The exhibition created the opportunity for them to make a positive contribution and to view themselves not only as professional learners but also as professional artists and critics who can contribute to our collective critical knowledge of how art interprets change and we interpret art. It is significant that the pupil who contributed to the exhibition and wrote in the visitor's book calls herself an 'artist'.

The exhibition was also a powerful opportunity for connecting learning, both as process and product, to participation in community life. By engaging in activities that had a social aim, the children who contributed to the exhibition saw their work as part of their acquisition of the interests, culture and social aspects of community life. Significantly, the public who recorded their comments and thoughts in the visitors' book made the same connection.

It is also important for pupils' sense of themselves as learners to be sustained before and after transfer. Some EIC Partnerships have used EIC funding to develop innovative cross-phase work, where learning mentors are employed specifically to work with targeted pupils in primary school and then undertake some post-transfer work in secondary schools. Usually called 'transition learning mentors', this title blurs the useful distinction made by Galton *et al* between transfer and transition. Transition learning mentor posts are instigated to support transfer between primary and secondary school. Case study 17 shows a transition learning mentor using active and creative forms of learning that sustain the high levels of engagement and enjoyment of a group in primary school and continuing to support and guide them during their first term of secondary school.

Case study 17: 'Changes' – an interactive, digital cross-curriculum project supporting transfer at Chingford Hall Primary School

Chingford Hall Primary School employs a transition LM. She worked with a targeted group of pupils whose barriers to learning put them at constant risk of exclusion and whose behaviour caused concern. During Year 6, three children in this group had been excluded from the playground during lunchtime for a total of forty-one lunchtimes and from school for a total of five days. Their imminent transfer to secondary school needed to be seen as a positive experience.

The transition LM set out to create a group forum in which these pupils could comfortably discuss their feelings about the changes that affected their lives in the past, present and future. The group used a variety of methods to express and explore their feelings: poems, photographs, drawings and circle time games. The transition LM wanted to create something lasting from the group – something the children could feel proud of and that the school could value them for.

The transition LM worked in partnership with the City Learning Centre to help the group create an interactive slide show of their photographs. These were scanned onto a disc and incorporated into a slide show with music. The task took six weeks and the transition LM worked with the group at the City Learning Centre for three hours each week. The children had the chance to use and develop their individual learning styles and ICT skills in an exciting but non-threatening environment.

The finished product was screened at the school's leavers' assembly and at parents' evening. The children's creations received much praise and positive feedback from staff, parents and the community. They were very proud of their work and visibly more confident and enthusiastic about transferring to secondary school.

The school was inspected by Ofsted during this time. The professional judgement of the inspectors, recorded in the school's inspection report, is: 'The efforts and participation of pupils was first rate and the slide show is of very good quality, showing an in-depth understanding of the changes that occur in the lives of young people.'

In the first term in secondary school, the transition LM spent time with these children offering them support and guidance and sharing with secondary colleagues important information about successful strategies and ways of working with them. Not a single one of these children has had difficulties during the transfer.

This case study reflects the importance of transfer to secondary school as a 'status passage' involving both continuity and change. It debunks the myth of the 'fresh start'. Far more instructive is an exchange of useful information between schools and sustaining pupils' sense of themselves as professional learners. As Galton observed (unpublished presentation) there has to be a ritual, a marked change – but there must also be some continuity. The first term of secondary school should be seen not as a settling-in period, but as an introduction to how secondary school will build on the learning journey – an introduction to how the school will continue to value its pupils as professional learners.

The ability to engage in sustained learning as a professional learner in the context of personal growth may well be the kind of education that will best prepare young people for life in a knowledge society. Scardamalia and Bereiter (1991, 1996, cited in Daniels, 2001: 103) aver that the skills that will prepare children for life in a knowledge society include flexibility, creativity, problem-solving ability, technological literacy, information-finding skills and a lifelong readiness to learn. Case study 17 illustrates working alliances in which at least the first four of these skills are developed.

This is not to say that learning mentors or even transition learning mentors are the whole solution to issues around transfer and transition. Where problems are rooted in school structures and cultures, they cannot create the solutions on their own. But they can be an effective, innovative part of solutions to the endemic issue of continuity and change at transfer that affect pupils' learning and participation at secondary school.

Another model of transition learning mentoring that has been effective is that of CEA @ Islington, which employs a transition learning mentor centrally to support issues of transfer between primary and secondary school. She works in a cluster of three primary schools, all with high pupil mobility, a high proportion of ethnic minority pupils and many pupils for whom English is an additional language. The transition learning mentor works in each of the primary schools prior to transfer and retains a caseload of three or four pupils in each school. Following transfer, she works with the pupils in their secondary school. Pupils are exited from the programme once an agreed support plan is in place.

Case study 18 demonstrates the impact of the transition learning mentor's work with one child and indicates how learning mentors support professional learning in the context of personal growth. It highlights the importance of seeing every child holistically and appreciating their ecological environments and the impact these have on learning and participation. This is particularly true when difficulties are compounded by having to manage the transfer to secondary school and all this involves. Although Jay was clearly making progress in his learning, he was being turned off school and beginning to disengage. It was probably only a matter of time before Jay's learning would

Case study 18: The importance of pupil 'choice and voice'

Jay is a twelve-year old boy in the care of the local authority. He has spent two years in long-term foster care and his siblings are in separate foster placements, awaiting adoption. Jay's foster placement is in another London borough so he has to travel for an hour and a half to and from school each day. It was decided that when he began secondary school it should be near his foster placement.

In primary school, Jay was attaining within the national average, but worked hard to do so. He had a steady group of friends. At his primary school, the transition LM worked with Jay for two sessions per week, one focused on building trust, encouraging him to share his feelings and build his confidence and the other focused on transfer and the changes Jay could expect.

When Jay transferred to his new secondary school in a different and rather distant London borough, the transition LM continued to work with him. Jay was offered support from his Head of Year and the transition LM found the new school flexible and supportive.

The new school and the transition LM were both concerned that Jay did not make friends and seemed lonely and isolated. He talked to classmates during lessons but did not try to establish friendships. He said he was worried about his peers finding out about his home life. Although Jay appeared to be making good progress in his learning, his increasing isolation and disengagement from his peers remained cause for concern.

Jay finally found a way of saying that he wanted to move home and school. Following further investigation, it was discovered that his foster placement had broken down. The transition LM was able to advocate for Jay. She felt strongly that if Jay were to face more change in his life, he should have some control over it. Plans were made for a new foster placement and for him to go to the secondary school he had always wanted to attend. The transition LM describes the change in Jay as 'someone switching the lights back on'.

suffer. If the transition learning mentor had not provided continuity across his educational settings and a relationship of trust, supported by skilled problem-management and advocacy, Jay might not have had the confidence to speak out and make his wants and needs heard. The transition learning mentor helped Jay to understand change and his rights as a looked after child and to manage his feelings. She contextualised her support for him in terms of his right to exercise some control over his life and in terms of supporting his personal growth. Thus she helped develop his ability to meet the personal challenge he was facing and build a purposeful and fulfilling life.

Personalised learning should support young people so they have a voice, and it should make services more responsive to users (see chapter two). This case study exemplifies Leadbeater's concept of personalised learning as 'intimate consultation': a learning mentor working with a pupil to help unlock their needs, preferences and aspirations through extended dialogue – a dialogue that in Jay's case extended across educational settings and even London boroughs. Without this work Jay's gradual disengagement from school would almost certainly have been misinterpreted, and the end result would have been grim.

So far I have focused on transfer between primary and secondary schools. But 'attention needs to be directed more evenly across the whole of the middle years of each phase of schooling as pupils move from one year to another' (Galton *et al*, 1999: v). These authors refer to a study by the NFER on children's performance in reading, spelling, written and mental maths on 'optional tests' designed to track pupils in Years 3, 4 and 5. They draw on indirect evidence from about twenty studies intended to establish the effects of initiatives with 'slow readers'. They conclude that the brief review 'does seem to underline the value of intervening at a fairly early stage in some pupils' careers post Key Stage 1 if they are to make expected levels of progress at Key Stage 2' (Galton *et al*, 1999: 7). Case study 19 highlights the need for further investigation into the effect of transfer and transitions at an even earlier age. It also demonstrates the impact of a learning mentor's support for a child's understanding of the social aspects of learning.

Case study 19: Supporting transitions in early learning – Henry Maynard Infant School

Henry Maynard Infant School employs two LMs. One focuses on the Foundation Stage and the other on Key Stage 1.

Stephen, whose behaviour had been very disruptive in the early learning environment, made a relatively successful but heavily supported transfer from nursery to reception. This support continued throughout his reception year, but with the transition to Key Stage 1 approaching with its change in curriculum and daily routines, Stephen's parents and the school were concerned. In order to ensure continuity from reception to Key Stage 1, the Key Stage 1 LM picked up the one-to-one mentoring support in his last term of reception. Her aim was to build a positive relationship with him and then support him through the transition to Key Stage 1. She also wanted to promote his independence in the classroom and reduce his disruptive and aggressive behaviour towards his peers.

As the LM had worked with Stephen and his family in reception, she developed a good understanding of his academic abilities and the social and emotional barriers to his learning. Knowing his strengths and weaknesses enabled her to share important information with his new class teacher and learning support assistant. They worked together to include him in activities that would promote positive outcomes. They developed a range of reward and incentive programmes in the classroom. The LM also offered small group work support for his learning and social development. She worked closely with his parents to evaluate and reflect on progress and discuss any difficulties that arose. A positive and healthy start to the day was offered through a place in the breakfast club as his family was having difficulty getting him to school in the mornings.

The LMs run an innovative playground activity programme at the school supported by other members of staff. The LM who was working with Stephen ensured that staff in the playground promoted positive relationships and play. Incidents of challenging behaviour were rigorously monitored and recorded. The school also offered Stephen a place on the play scheme co-ordinated by the LMs during the school holidays, giving his family some much needed time out and also building his social skills with other children.

The LM recognised the need to signpost other services to the family. She made a referral to the local Child and Family Consultation Service, with a view to supporting Stephen's parents with behaviour strategies in the home.

The outcome of all these interventions has been a good transition. Stephen's attitude towards school is far more positive and there are more good days than bad. Support in the classroom has been withdrawn as he is more independent in class. The reward sessions are still very much a feature of support, but the one-to-one mentoring sessions have been gradually reduced. Stephen has made good progress in his learning and can complete work unaided. He has also made progress in understanding the social nature of learning: he has much better relationships with his peers and his class teacher and generally adheres to classroom rules. In the playground, he is reported to be quite a popular play time buddy.

The effective practice of the LMs at Henry Maynard Infant has been recognised by Ofsted. The school's 2004 inspection report commented:

> All staff work very effectively in helping pupils who have experienced disorder or disruption in their lives to develop confidence and self-esteem so that they, too, play a full part in the school community. The school's two learning mentors carry out an important role here. Their well-run breakfast sessions provide a comforting and well-organised start to the day as well as reducing lateness and improving attitudes to learning. Learning mentors provide specific support for pupils... mostly on a one-to-one basis that helps them with their personal and emotional development.

This learning mentor took care to develop a holistic under-standing of the child in the different contexts in which he lives. She worked with the family, building trust, acceptance and empathic understanding, and brokered support for them while working with the class teacher and ensuring targeted interventions to dismantle social, emotional and behavioural barriers. All these interventions were aimed at supporting Stephen as a learner, within the context of his personal growth.

There is little practice guidance on learning mentoring in foundation and infant sectors and much more is needed. Case study 19 goes some way towards modelling learning mentoring as the facilitation of learning through personal and social growth. In all learning mentoring, but perhaps most acutely in the early years, this facilitation or personalisation of learning relies not just on the personal relationship between child and adult but also on the capacity of the learning mentor to form professional and supportive relationships with the other adults in the child's life.

This chapter has so far considered one of the detailed functions – assisting children and young people to make a successful transfer or transition – within the broader function of providing a complementary service. Next I explore how learning mentors can 'contribute to the comprehensive assessment of children and young people entering educational establishments and the review of their progress and learning' (Sauvé Bell, 2003: 19). There is some overlap in these two functions, as pupils transferring between educational establishments are also entering a new school, so I concentrate on mid-term entrants or mobile pupils.

Enhancing arrangements to support pupils entering or returning to school

In guidance on *Managing Pupil Mobility* the then Secretary of State for Education observed that there are many different types of mobile pupils

> ...from refugees and asylum seekers who arrive in the country with little or no understanding of English, to children of armed forces families, children whose parents may have been separated, children who have been abused and those why may have changed school because of issues such as bullying. (DfES, 2003c: 3)

In the report *Pupil Mobility in Schools* (2000), Janet Dobson identifies four categories of mobility: international migration, encompassing labour or career cycles and refugees; internal migration, encompassing labour or career cycles and young people from travelling families; institutional movement, including exclusions and voluntary transfers; and individual movement, including looked after children and the fragmentation of families.

Significantly, the guidance contextualises mobility in terms of recognising and celebrating the strengths of mobile communities. In identifying some of the challenges of pupil mobility, the guidance states that 'mobile pupils are particularly worried about integrating with the new community and will be concerned about how they will be received and whether they will have to cope with bullying or racial abuse because at the outset they have limited peer support' (Dobson *et al*, 2000: 13). Learning mentors have a role in welcoming pupils who arrive mid-term and in helping them manage these feelings and anxieties. Interestingly, the guidance frames schools' obligations to support this group of pupils as '...a moral responsibility to maximise the opportunities and progress of the individual, whatever the duration of their stay, and an obligation to manage the exit process well to facilitate a successful start in the receiving school' (*ibid*, 2000: 19).

For children from refugee and travelling families, there is an additional 'moral obligation' on schools to oppose the racism promulgated by the media and promote genuine inclusion. In unpublished training materials, Tim Spafford and Bill Bolloten point out that refugees are not a homogenous group. They vary in how they cope with adversity, and the political situations they are fleeing vary. Like Egan, Spafford and Bolloten do not encourage schools to see refugee children as helpless victims. They emphasise instead their resourcefulness and recommend opportunity development, participatory approaches and resilience-building.

Children and young people from travelling families are likewise not a homogenous group. Guidance on raising the achievement of pupils from Gypsy Traveller families emphasises raising the profile of race equality within schools and 'addressing their social as well as academic needs' (DfES, 2003a: 5).

Learning mentors can play a significant role in welcoming those who enter school mid-term including refugees and those from travelling families. It should not be assumed that these pupils will necessarily need additional support. What learning mentors provide is a point of contact, should problem situations arise.

Case study 20 shows how one school deploys their learning mentors as part of their welcome to new arrivals and how they are supported, where appropriate, to negotiate the social context of school.

Case study 20: Welcoming and working with pupils admitted mid-term to Tom Hood School

Tom Hood is in an area with high mobility. Most weeks there are one or two admissions and the school has good procedures for welcoming these pupils. LMs see all mid-term admissions after they have been at the school for a couple of weeks.

Each pupil is given an individual appointment. They have the opportunity to discuss why they have moved to the school and their feelings about the transfer. The LM looks at any issues that have arisen for them since joining the school. Pupils are invited to talk about their work and organisational issues and their relationships with peers and adults in the school. The discussions focus on helping pupils to look at what is going well for them and finding strategies to deal with some of the hurdles they are facing. All pupils are given information about the role of the LM and how the LM programme may be of use to them in the future. LMs give feedback from these meetings to form tutors, heads of year and special educational needs co-ordinators.

Mid-term admission interviews are often followed up with practical issues. One pupil who was having difficulty in completing homework due to circumstances at home was taken on a tour of the school by the LM to determine where he could find homework clubs and extra-curricular ICT facilities. Another pupil joined Tom Hood after having been out of school for four months following difficulties with her peers at her previous school. At the initial meeting she appeared to be settling in well but the LM felt there could be difficulties later. So she was offered a follow up appointment two weeks later which she accepted. The LM continued to monitor her and when the form tutor became aware of some issues within the peer group, she was offered a regular mentoring session. The early contact with this pupil enabled proactive measures to be taken.

Another pupil, Kerry, returned to the school after time elsewhere. When previously at the school she had been involved in fights and was concerned lest such behaviour would still be expected of her. She was encouraged to plan how she might deal with such situations. A week later, Kerry came back to see the LM as she was having difficulties with another girl. Kerry used the LM to give herself some time out. The LM and the head of year provided a forum for discussion that enabled the girls to sort out their differences and avoid fighting.

These case studies indicate how learning mentors can complement existing school provision and contribute to supporting pupils when they enter or return to school. The next examples show how learning mentoring can complement a range of other provision in school.

Programme development

Learning mentors can complement existing provision by providing a range of strategies and programmes for overcoming barriers to learning and participation, including:

- contributing to the provision made by a school for the highly able and pupils with special abilities who are underachieving

- enhancing pastoral arrangements and contributing to raising achievement by working with pupils who experience barriers in relation to behaviour, motivation, aspirations and academic achievement

- implementing strategies for ensuring that all children and young people are given access to learning mentoring

- contributing to schools' capacity to support their pupils to learn more effectively.

Contributing to provision for highly able pupils who are underachieving

Just as schools must provide support for pupils whose attainment is below that of their peers, so must they provide for able pupils. The Excellence in Cities programme has funded some schools to make this provision under the gifted and talented strand. The Excellence in Cities definition of gifted and talented is the top five to ten percent of any cohort. Within this group, it is expected that two-thirds will be gifted or academically very able and the rest will be talented or have abilities in a particular field. This strand of Excellence in Cities has attracted strong criticism for creating an elite cadre of young people, often from socio-economically privileged families and affording them additional privileges. However, this can be an equal opportunities argument (see Winstanley, 2004 and the PISA findings in chapter three of this book). Schools with a strong equality ethos ensure that the gifted and talented cohort is rigorously monitored in terms of gender, ethnicity and economic deprivation indices, such free school meals. These schools recognise that many young people from economically deprived backgrounds may not be achieving as well as they can, so may not automatically qualify for the top five to ten percent in terms of their academic achievement. Schools have developed ways of identifying such pupils, ensuring that their gifted and talented provision is part of their broader aim to promote equal opportunity and narrow the achievement gap.

According to Teare (1997), able underachievers show characteristics such as:

- a marked difference between the quality of their oral and written work
- starting a task well but leaving it unfinished or rushing it as concentration diminishes
- being bored for much of the time but showing odd flashes of brilliance when interested
- being hypercritical of efforts of themselves and others
- performing noticeably better in just one or two areas where their relationship with the teacher is good
- showing dislike of routine tasks but sometimes sparkling when the work is more unusual
- asking challenging questions that show perception and intelligence but not always for the right reasons.

Some schools ensure that the learning mentor programme complements gifted and talented provision by targeting the highly able who are underachieving. These pupils often have social and emotional needs, difficulties with peers or problems managing the expectations of teachers and parents. They may feel anxious or isolated and have low self-esteem and little confidence about their ability. The aim of learning mentor provision is to create a means of providing stimulating experiences for these pupils, while also exploring their sense of themselves as learners. In case study 21 we see how the learning mentor contributed to identifying one pupil's special talent.

Case study 21: Unearthing special talents and abilities at Mission Grove Primary School

The LM at Mission Grove Primary School worked with a child identified as underachieving academically. Tony had little confidence in his abilities as a learner and at times behaved in challenging and disruptive ways which caused the staff concern.

The LM decided to focus on Tony's anger and self-esteem and planned a number of interventions. She invited him to a puzzle-club during lunchtime, to which he brought a friend; she gave him additional responsibilities to help him feel important and she offered one-to-one mentoring sessions. She also maintained regular communication with his mother and had weekly meetings with her to share information and acknowledge his successes.

The LM sought to build an intervention around something Tony genuinely enjoyed doing. Through their conversations, she learned that he enjoyed music and was good at dancing. She had just started a school dance club, so she invited him, initially to help with the music, but after a couple of weeks he started joining in. He was obviously really good and when she realised this she encouraged him to audition for the school's production of *Bugsy Malone*. He landed a leading role in the production and showed confidence in learning his words and in performing. He ended up being one of the stars of the show!

Through the work of the LM, the school recognised Tony's special talent and he is now on the gifted and talented register. He recently attended a special drama course and is much more confident about his creative talents.

The recognition of his abilities has also enhanced his confidence in himself as a learner. He is now motivated to achieve in class and his teacher commented that his determination and motivation have been an inspiration to others. He is predicted to achieve level 4 in Maths and level 5 in English and Science.

Through the working alliance with Tony, the learning mentor explores his interests and strengths. As in many of the other cases described, she does not focus only on problems or difficulties. By creating opportunities for Tony, the learning mentor uncovered a genuine dramatic talent. However, a word of caution to the over-zealous: mentoring is a genuinely free relationship and every young person has the right to choose whether or not, and how, they develop their gifts and talents.

Another school has deployed their learning mentor to improve the confidence of able children by using a 'philosophy for children' approach to develop their thinking skills.

Case study 22: A philosophy group at Greenleaf Primary School

The LM at Greenleaf Primary School identified two children who appeared to be dissociated with the learning in the classroom, so put little effort into their work and were perceived to be underachieving. The LM put them into a group with two highly able children who were working to their potential.

The LM selected material from *The Philosophy Files* (Law, 2000). He focused on the chapter dealing with where right and wrong come from. The group discussed various aspects of the chapter each week over six weeks. The LM stressed that there were no right or wrong answers. At the end of each session, he asked the group to think about an issue raised by the text over the coming week. At the end of the six sessions, he set the group the task of constructing their own theory of morality.

At first the two children who were working to their potential were the most responsive during the sessions – though not necessarily the best thinkers. However, over the weeks, the two perceived to be underachieving became comfortable with the structure of the group and performed much better. As their confidence in their ability to think philosophically grew, so their performance in the classroom and their learning improved.

The philosophy group creates a social and participative space in which children are encouraged to develop thinking tools. The learning mentor acts as the philosophy discourse guide, supporting the group in collective and philosophical ways of thinking together. He uses question-and-answer sessions to develop understanding, focusing on problem-exploration together and trying to make sense of collective social experience – what Mercer (2000, cited in Daniels, 2001: 123) calls developing children's capacity to be 'interthinkers'. Significantly, the learning mentor brings an inclusive, equalities-led focus to the philosophy group by including two underachieving able children, in an attempt to help them perceive themselves as successful learners and also as young philosophers.

Case study 23: Able children leading learning – T-shirt printing at Worth Valley Primary School

The LM at Worth Valley Primary School has an interest in ICT and art and design. Following a digital video project, she designed and implemented a T-shirt printing project. The Year 4 class selected to take part had had several supply teachers over the course of the year and the Headteacher wanted a specific long term project that would give the class a clear focus and a more positive outlook.

The project took place during curriculum time in Art and ICT lessons. There was a wide range of abilities in the class of 26, including children in the gifted and talented cohort as well as children who were being mentored. They used the ICT suite when developing designs, and parents were involved in selecting pictures and logos.

The individual ICT and design technology skills required to complete the project were considerable. The children were working at Level 3 in National Curriculum terms in ICT, Design Technology and Art – well beyond age-related expectations.

One of the most interesting aspects of the project was how much peer support took place among the children. An ethos of team effort developed, which was precisely the aim of the project!

Some schools ensure that their gifted and talented provision is part of their broader focus on equal opportunity by deploying the resources of children identified as highly able or having special abilities to support others.

Case study 23 demonstrates not only how the skilled deployment of able children can support learning and equality of opportunity in the classroom, but also the role of learning mentors in whole-school improvement. The skills of the Worth Valley learning mentor supported a whole class whose learning had been disrupted by the constant change of teachers. Her work with this class demonstrates her understanding of the value of learning as social practice. Lack of teacher continuity had disrupted the social processes of the classroom and the class lacked focus and needed an intervention that re-established learning as social practice – and that is what the T-shirt printing project achieved.

Enhancing pastoral arrangements

The outcomes framework in *Every Child Matters: Change for Children* (DfES: 2004e) states that children and young people have the right to make positive contributions to their school and communities, and that judgements will be made on how schools help young people to develop socially and emotionally. In case study 24, the learning mentor provided a range of interventions and programmes designed to complement the work of pastoral staff to support the social and emotional development of a group of Year 8 pupils. The learning mentor helped the group to overcome barriers to learning and participation in relation to behaviour, motivation, aspirations and academic achievement.

Bayley and Haddock (1999) argue for an interactive and dynamic understanding of behaviour, located in classroom processes and relationships (see chapter four). There is no 'good' or 'bad' behaviour – there is only an understanding of productive and unproductive ways of behaving.

Case study 24: Drama and dialogue as dialectic tools for change at Warwick School for Boys

From a range of school data: performance on standardised tests, behaviour monitoring records and incident logs, the Head of Year 8 and Learning Support Unit Manager at Warwick School for Boys identified nine boys who would benefit from access to the LM. All the boys were believed to be under-achieving and had a history of being disruptive or distracted in lessons. These boys were increasingly disengaging from learning, displaying signs of low self-esteem, and most lacked supportive peer relationships and had been persistent victims of bullying. They also displayed low emotional coping abilities.

The primary aim of the LM was to develop supportive and positive relationships by creating a non-threatening environment that would generate trust and the potential for improved learning and participation. He also aimed to develop and improve the boys' sense of value and trust in themselves by empowering them to utilise their own attributes to bring about positive change.

Each boy was offered a weekly one-to-one session of 45 minutes. The boys also came together as a group for an hour once a week. The sessions had clear and structured objectives, but there was also room for flexibility of the kind that is difficult to create in mainstream classes. The one-to-one sessions took the form of discussions and practical activities like study skills or focused learning tasks, role play exercises that reflected prevailing issues, and recognising triggers, non-aggressive alternatives and assertive responses. This created a non-threatening and safe space for each boy to talk about his feelings and resolve some emotional conflicts. In the sessions they could have their individual needs met. They could reflect on their behaviours and how this affected others. It allowed the LM to give specific positive feedback without embarrassing the boys and helped them to achieve a more realistic self-image.

The group sessions were needed to enhance appropriate peer group interactions in a structured and safe setting. All the boys participated in short programmes of activities designed to focus on social and interpersonal skills. Tasks involved taking turns or co-operating with each other and gave them the chance to explore different ways of responding or dealing with situations. They received appropriate guidance from each other, and promoted self-recognition of their achievements. They focused on their similarities and explored and shared ideas about ways of retaining control. Pressures that made learning more difficult were identified, such as fighting for status in the pecking order of their peer group. They explored how their dislike of certain teachers impeded their learning and saw that some disruptive behaviour is motivated by revenge – wanting to make a teacher feel as small or angry or bad as they felt themselves. As the group work progressed, it became clear that all the boys expressed emotional difficulties and conflicts through their behaviour in one way or another.

The LM used his own background in drama to focus the work and used role play and improvisation. This allowed the boys to empathise in situations they were encountering in school. They practised using assertive responses in a variety of scenarios, and learned to replace aggression with assertion. They practised dealing with conflict in the classroom, resisting peer pressure to behave in unproductive ways, and strove to ignore distractions and deal with bullying. The drama and role-play revealed how some of the boys' behaviours affected others. Circle-time activities also helped build self-esteem and improve their self-confidence.

Throughout the programme, the LM maintained close contact with the families of every pupil in this group.

As the work developed, the LM made additional interventions. He provided an informal lunchtime drop-in'club which almost all the boys in the group used, although it was open to other pupils too. This helped to ease their interactions with other boys and was instrumental in improving their confidence so that they eventually participated fully in recreational periods.

The LM also set up a catch-up club so that the boys who had been withdrawn from mainstream lessons did not fall too far behind in their learning. This was supported by the Learning

Support Unit Manager who gave his time and teaching skills to the project. So the boys had focused one-to-one learning time without the constraints of peer pressure and could work at their own pace.

One boy improved from level 3 in English to level 5 and three others' subject levels also improved.

The LM reflects that his interventions with this group were intended to make a difference to specific issues and not to general behaviour. He aimed to change the boys' personal perceptions by developing their self-awareness and personal growth. This encouraged them to take responsibility for how they behaved. Focusing the boys on simple tasks, such as getting a target booked signed by teachers, meant a step towards personal achievement. The simple tasks and small steps motivated them to take greater responsibility, showed them they could change their behaviour and increased their self-worth.

The work of the learning mentor in case study 24 focused on the social processes in the classroom and how the pupils relate to each other and the teacher. His work was practical and collaborative. It sought to change specific unproductive and unsatisfying behaviour towards others, rather than positioning the boys as problems, so it helped them reflect critically on their behaviour, motivations and aspirations. Drama and role-play were used as a dialectic tool, investigating real situations of conflict in an attempt to bring about change. By focusing on each boy's personal growth, the learning mentor brought about positive change in their sense of themselves as learners and this assisted their learning.

Implementing strategies for ensuring that all pupils have access to learning mentoring

In all the cases described so far, referrals into the learning mentor programme have come from adults. However, many learning mentors try in principle to provide access to learning mentor support for all pupils who wish to refer themselves.

Case study 25: Talk Time at Sybourn Junior School

The LM at Sybourn Junior was concerned that pupils had no opportunity to refer themselves to the service she provides. She investigated the idea of a drop-in lunchtime club but thought it would not allow children to discuss anything that was worrying them in private. And a lunchtime club would attract children who were bored in the playground or whose friends attended or because they didn't like the cold.

The LM developed the idea of Talk Time. Talk Time appointments are scheduled for 15 minutes during the morning break so are not during lesson time. She makes it clear to children that to have an appointment, they have to give up their own time. She produced Talk Time request slips and appointment cards and put up posters around the school and a letterbox for the children to post their Talk Time request slips. She made arrangements to speak to all Year 5 and 6 classes individually to explain what Talk Time is and how they could use it. Any child who wants to make an appointment fills in a request slip and posts it in the box. She collects the requests from the box and makes the appointments. The child receives an appointment card in a sealed envelope telling them when and where to come. They can come alone or with a friend. Each teacher agreed to keep Talk Time slips in their classroom.

The LM was careful to announce the Talk Time service to parents and families, sending a letter to each family with children in Years 5 and 6. Parents can refuse permission for their child to access the service.

Talk Time is amazingly popular in the school. The way the children use the service has become increasingly sophisticated. They discuss things that are worrying or confusing them, seek help to understand and manage a bereavement or illness or to explore academic or friendship issues. The LM reflects that where conflict resolution has been discussed, there has been immense emotional growth. It is accepted that Talk Time is not about telling tales but about positively resolving issues and building stronger friendships. Children have become more able to resolve issues for themselves using strategies they have experienced during Talk Time.

Talk Time has also been invaluable in creating a safe environment in which to disclose problems of bullying. Several children raised this issue and the LM has arranged bullying prevention workshops in certain classes. Thus Talk Time has resulted in developmental work that is now helping create a better social environment in the whole school.

Case study 25 describes one innovative and highly effective self-referral tool. It shows how a self-referral tool can enable children to take responsibility for personalising their learning by seeking their own intimate consultation.

Contributing to a school's capacity to enhance pupils' learning

In all the case studies, the link between the psychological and social aspects of learning is clear. The programmes learning mentors have developed to complement existing activity in school are in response to perceived barriers to learning and participation. The last two case studies in this chapter show learning mentors contributing to specific programmes which support pupils to *learn* more effectively. These programmes are less about barriers and more to do with encouraging the joy of learning. Case studies 26 and 27 show how learning mentors have engaged children's imagination and creativity through reading.

The learning mentor in case study 26 uses her own creative skills to help children learn. Not only has she complemented existing arrangements for children to learn more effectively, but she has created a new and innovative way of raising achievement in the school through reading.

In equally successful ways, the learning mentors at Henry Maynard Infant School and St Margaret of Antioch's Primary School have made incalculable contributions to creating reading cultures in their schools. Theirs is not a narrow, instrumentalist

Case study 26: Making story sacks at Henry Maynard Infant School

The LM at Henry Maynard Infant School attended a course on how to use story sacks. When she set out to buy ready-made professionally produced story sacks, she found they were far too expensive so she decided to make her own.

First, she chose a popular book: *The Hungry Caterpillar* by Eric Carle. She then decided on two sets of visual aids: felt, cut into the food shapes with a hole in the middle for a caterpillar to be threaded through; and play food props. She also included a factual book on the life cycle of caterpillars, a hologram book on butterflies, a crazy caterpillar game, finger puppet templates, a matching memory-game made from Clip-art on the computer, and sequencing sheets. She purchased many of these resources from car boot sales. The sack to keep everything in is an old pillowcase with a drawstring tie.

The LM has now made eight story sacks, each for a different book, and each costing about £10.

She believes that children find story sacks motivational, creative and imaginative tools. They capture the creativity that schools are trying to introduce into the curriculum. They fascinate children who show little interest in reading books and help introduce them to a culture of reading for pleasure and interest. The sacks are a way of engaging children in stories and books in ways that involve not only reading but creative activity. The activities can be used in a cross-curricular way to build knowledge about the world: science, history, literature and the world of ideas. Story sacks can also enhance language, social skills, listening skills and basic skills.

view of reading. Reading engages children – and in case study 27, the whole school and community – in a world of ideas, literature, history, imagination and creative thought.

Case study 27: Reading journeys at St Margaret of Antioch's Primary School

An innovative reading project by the LM at St Margaret of Antioch's Primary School encouraged everyone in the school community to dedicate quality time to reading. The project set out to increase children's interest in books and reading and create opportunities for parents to be actively involved in their children's education. The school also tried to enrich children's reading experiences through exposing them to a wide range of performers and artists.

In the eight-stage journey, children tackled different targets at each stage. Nursery and Infant-aged children read or had read to them twenty books per stage. Year 3 and 4 children read two hundred pages per stage while those in Years 5 and 6 read two hundred and fifty pages. Adults read three hundred pages per stage. Eighty-five children and forty-three adults embarked on the journey.

Funding from Dingle Toxeth Granby's Education Action Zone, Toxeth Education Trust and Liverpool Housing Association enabled the school to give children incentive prizes at a weekly achievement assembly, as they reached each stage of the journey.

The four-month programme began with a launch day when Dance in Education presented *Bookworm's Marvellous Adventure* and a storyteller entertained the audience with tales from around the world. There followed a weekly family reading club for Key Stage 1 children and their parents after school – magazines and books were supplied for the adults to read.

The reading journey featured a book fair and an artist-in-residence who made models of fantastical creatures and dream catchers with the children. Art clubs were devoted to making book illustrations. Some children read plays and acted them out with a teacher.

Members of the Royal Liverpool Philharmonic Orchestra visited the school and played the children and adults a medley of songs linking music to traditional stories. A Read-In was held for Red Nose Day and a group of children read an

afternoon away at a local bookshop. The children and staff together read 8,050 pages and raised £55 pounds for the charity.

The project has had effects of various kinds. Parents swapped
books at the breakfast club and discussed their opinions
about them. Nursery staff have noticed that children are using
the library area more. At the time of writing, nursery and Key
Stage 1 children have read a total of 4,840 books. Children in
the junior school have read 33,215 pages and adults 59,365
pages. But it is not the number of pages or books that count –
it is the reading journey.

This chapter has illustrated some of the many ways in which
learning mentors provide complementary services to schools.
The case studies demonstrate how learning mentors enhance
existing provision and how they innovate to improve schools'
capacity to support learning and participation for all pupils,
from the highly able to the disengaged. We see practice-based
evidence of active and creative forms of learning. We see how
learning mentors improve social processes in schools and thus
encourage social inclusion. Education must enable young
people to engage positively and confidently with social and cultural change (Robinson *et al*, 2001). But it must also meet the
personal challenge and 'develop the unique capacities of all
young people and to provide a basis on which they can build
lives that are purposeful and fulfilling' (Robinson *et al*, 2001: 18-
25). The government believes that schools must therefore per-
sonalise learning. The learning mentors discussed here have re-
introduced the person, and the community, into personalised
learning, in powerful and creative ways. The final chapter shows
how learning mentors work in a wide range of networks.

10

Working within an extended range of networks

This final chapter is devoted to examples of how learning mentors 'work within an extended range of networks and partnerships to broker support and learning opportunities and improve the quality of services to children and young people' (Sauvé Bell: 2003: 10). *The Functional Map for the Provision of Learning Mentor Services* divides this into three detailed functions. Learning mentors:

■ develop and maintain appropriate contact with the families and carers of pupils who have identified needs

■ negotiate, establish and maintain effective working partnerships with other agencies and individuals in order to address pupils' needs and help remove barriers to their learning

■ contribute to the identification and sharing of good practice between individuals and partner agencies to enhance mentoring provision.

Working with families
Before they begin working with pupils, learning mentors obtain the permission of parents or carers. They actively seek to in-

volve parents and carers in the process. As a minimum, they involve families in ecological assessment and action planning, respecting the valuable knowledge the parents and carers have about their child.

Case study 24 (p175-177) described how the learning mentor at Warwick School for Boys planned interventions with a group of boys in Year 8 who were experiencing barriers to learning because of their behaviour, motivation, aspirations or academic achievement. He used drama and dialogue in one-to-one and group settings to change unproductive and unsatisfying ways of interacting with others. This learning mentor describes how he worked with one pupil and his family.

Case study 28: Including families in problem-management – Warwick School for Boys

One pupil in the group became overwhelmed and distressed because of issues of puberty and difficulties in relationships with his family. He felt pressure by his family members to live up to their expectations. Transference from this caused conflicts with his parents and teachers.

The LM worked hard to develop a good relationship with the family, built on trust and respect, and worked with them to help develop their understanding of the pressures their child was experiencing. He discussed the possibility of self-referring to the Family Service Unit. The family saw this as a way of taking responsibility for and managing the relationship difficulties themselves. They accepted the referral form and sought his help to fill it out.

This learning mentor viewed the pupil's family not as part of the problem but as part of the solution. He does not rush to judgement but suggests an external agency they might seek help from, without imposing it as a solution. He respects their need for self-determination and assumes they have the resources to change if they choose to. He shares the helping process with them and acts as a consultant to them, supporting their completion of the referral form, not doing it for them. This is indeed skilled helping!

It is not just in the one-to-one process that learning mentors can broker opportunities for parents. Parents and families are among the networks with whom learning mentors can work in other ways to broker more generic opportunities. The learning mentor at Sybourn Junior enabled access to learning mentoring to all children in Year 5 and 6 through her Talk Time programme. In the following case study, the learning mentor at a secondary school implements a similar initiative for parents.

Case study 29: Talk Time for parents at Norlington School

The LM at Norlington wrote to the parents of all Year 7 and Year 8 pupils to offer to discuss any aspect of their child's learning and participation if they made an appointment. Talk Time for Parents aims to give parents the message that the school values their child and values parents' involvement. The LM believes this is a way of working positively and pro-actively with parents, enabling them to talk to her before difficulties escalate into problems.

The meetings with parents are held in a comfortable quiet room, free from interruptions. Parents are respected as partners in their child's learning and participation at school.

Talk Time for Parents is still in the early stages. It has been well received by parents and the take-up has been good. The LM plans to extend the programme to offer monthly opportunities for parents to come together in a forum to share ideas. This will give isolated parents the opportunity to meet and network with other parents.

This innovative scheme provides parents with a non-threatening way of accessing their child's secondary school. It empowers them to initiate a dialogue more usually initiated by the school once problems exist. It provides a blame-free, solution-focused forum and establishes a working alliance between the parent and the learning mentor. It is collaborative by its very nature, keeps the parents' agenda rather than the school's in focus and assumes the parents' goodwill. The idea of bringing parents together in a forum to share ideas engages the community of parents as real partners in improving their children's learning and participation in school.

For some parents, it is the curriculum which is a barrier to their participation in their child's learning. Some learning mentors work with external agencies and community organisations to implement programmes for parents to enable them to keep up with their children. The learning mentor at Greenleaf Primary School arranged a programme of this kind, helping parents to understand the literacy and numeracy strategies (see chapter four). The programme was particularly successful for parents who were unfamiliar with the English education system.

Developing effective working partnerships with other agencies

One of the strengths of learning mentor programmes is that they provide a resource within the school to 'develop and maintain a comprehensive network of support agencies, individuals and opportunities which can assist children and young people' (Sauvé Bell, 2003: 12). The next four examples illustrate how learning mentors work within these extended partnerships to broker opportunities for children and young people. The first is a programme for young people who were underachieving and disengaged from school. The second shows how learning mentors established a partnership with a local health and social care service to provide additional forms of support in a multi-agency context. The third case study is of working with the statutory Youth Service to broker a wider range of mentoring experiences, with a strong focus on community mentoring. The fourth describes how learning mentors from two recently amalgamated schools worked together to create what they call 'a tale of two communities'.

Case study 30: Chingford Foundation School's 'Compact Club'

In 2001, the LM at Chingford Foundation School ran a pilot programme for pupils who needed extra support with basic skills and lacked motivation and confidence. These pupils were considered to be at risk of becoming disaffected. The LM approached a local organisation to co-facilitate the programme. Compact Club has been flourishing for three years.

Compact Club provides an accessible route to a national award. The Silver and Bronze Youth Award, accredited by ASDAN and designed to raise self-esteem and motivation, provides self-directed, active and creative learning opportunities or 'challenges' intended to make learning and achievement fun. Pupils must undertake fifteen challenges or tasks, each of at least four hours. Challenges are selected by the pupil and club leader together. They are linked to the National Curriculum but can be completed outside school.

The visits and activities to support the pupils' personal learning and development address citizenship and community issues. The idea is for the young people to make a positive contribution to school and society. For example, pupils undertook CPR training after hearing about the Ambulance Service on a visit to the Ambulance Museum. Others have taken part in Shopmobility, helping elderly people in the local area and assisting at the senior citizens' Christmas party. They have responded to Shoebox Christmas Appeal, providing shoeboxes filled with useful items and also helping at the Shoebox Appeal warehouse to pack the boxes to send to children in Eastern Europe. Other pupils have learned about procedures at the Magistrates' Court, Fire Service and Accident Prevention Service. Pupils have visited local Further Education Colleges where they were given mock interviews. An activity day at Herfordshire Young Mariners' Base developed their teamwork skills as they tackled raft-building and rock-climbing.

The LM reports that the programme is increasingly successful. In 2002/2003, all pupils in the programme took their GCSEs. Attendance levels were high, averaging 95 percent. Two pupils achieved 100 percent attendance. Eight of the fifteen pupils achieved the full award. Their self-confidence improved markedly and so did their social interactions with peers improved. The programme was evaluated along with the pupils, and 86 percent said they felt that they had fewer problems at school since joining Compact Club. Fourteen of the fifteen entered further education or employment on leaving school and the remaining pupil intends to enter further education this year.

Ofsted commented about the Compact Club in its inspection report of January 2004:

> The Compact Club caters for pupils in both Years 10 and 11 who follow the ASDAN challenge course, which enables these pupils to gain both Bronze and Silver awards. The pupils enjoy the course and the challenge that it gives them. It has given them self-esteem and the ability to work in groups. It prepares them well for college and employment... The learning mentor works well with Year 10 and 11 pupils at risk of becoming disaffected. They undertake a series of challenges, leading to the ASDAN silver award. The school is piloting an initiative for these awards to be recognised as a GCSE.

The awarding body, ASDAN, has recently announced that the Silver Award will qualify as equivalent to a GSCE grade D-G. Recognition of the Silver Award within the National Qualifications Framework will earn points in the school's attainment tables and will raise the profile of this intervention. The LM is hoping to take part in a pilot initiative to offer Compact Club as a full GCSE option.

Schools are expected to show how they support young people to achieve economic well-being by helping them to prepare for further education and employment (DfES: 2004e). As the case study shows, learning mentors can support this outcome. By working in partnership with an extended range of services and community and voluntary agencies in the local area, the learning mentor provides a programme which has a significant impact on young people identified as being at risk of disengaging from learning and participation.

The Compact Club model fits Egan's model of skilled-helping. It creates a structure within which young people can choose realistic but challenging goals that will help them explore opportunities and possibilities for a better future. Their individual learning programme, constituted by the fifteen challenges, is both a change agenda and an action plan. The club itself gives an incentive to commit to the programme and so do the early opportunities for success, something these pupils may not have experienced often. Compact Club is the epitome of a solution-focused programme, focusing not on problems or problem-management but on opportunities. A bit like the group work at Leytonstone School (case study 7, p128), Compact Club generates 'circle of courage' opportunities to develop a sense of belonging, generosity, independence and mastery. It quickly moves away from discourses of difficulty, deficits and risk associated with the referral into the programme into discourses of opportunity and success which draw on the personal strengths and resources of the participants.

Case study 31: A multi-agency partnership with a health and social care service at Tom Hood School

Tom Hood is an 'extended school' which means it offers an extended range of services in its community. The school employs a qualified and experienced counsellor who provides an excellent service to pupils. But there is a long waiting list and the pupils cannot self-refer to the counsellor.

The LMs at Tom Hood wanted to develop a multi-agency partnership with a local tier one/ two health and social care service for those aged 11 to 21 that provides counselling for young people but is based at the other end of the borough, making access difficult. The service is committed to working in sites that are accessible to their client-group, so was keen to offer sessions in the school.

The LMs were eager to take up this service but were aware that they needed to be sensitive about how they facilitated this complementary service to the existing provision. They arranged meetings with the deputy head teacher and the service manager to draw up a contract between the school and health and social care service so that the counsellor from the service was familiar with and would work within the school Child Protection procedures. They arranged for the school counsellor and the counsellor from the health and social care service to meet to discuss the models of counselling each practised and ensure that channels of communication were open and accessible.

Parents were informed of the service and the information available, about, for instance, the drop-in and self-referral options. Parents were invited to discuss any questions or concerns with the LMs or tell them if they did not want their child to have access to the service.

The LMs negotiated an additional morning of individual counselling sessions followed by a lunchtime drop in service, to be staffed by the service's counsellor and a nurse. Pupils were able to access information on issues including sexual and mental health. The school's governors agreed that if the professionals felt it was in the young person's best interest, free condoms and a pregnancy testing service could be provided.

The learning mentors at Tom Hood brought together education and health professionals from different backgrounds to provide a supportive service based on self-referral. This model of multi-agency working within an integrated framework on a school site reflects the emerging policy context set out in *Every Child Matters* and the Children Act (2004). The joint delivery of services here described leads to better accessibility to services and therefore better outcomes for children and young people.

The next case study reflects how learning mentors can develop effective links with statutory organisations. The learning mentor worked with the Youth Service to broker community mentoring experiences and thus enhance the range of mentoring provision within the school.

Case study 32: Brokering mentoring experiences within a community mentoring project at Walthamstow School for Girls

The assistant headteacher and the LM at Walthamstow School for Girls are both committed to community participation in supporting pupils. With the support of the senior leadership team, the LM approached the local youth service about starting a community mentoring programme. The youth service had a new policy: their youth workers were offering mentoring within the community, including schools. The LM saw this as a chance to strengthen mentoring provision in the school, which she recognised she could not do alone.

The LM has worked with the community mentoring project for four years now. The youth service carry out the police checks and offer training and supervision of their staff on the community mentoring project. Youth workers offer one-to-one mentoring with young people identified as underachieving. Twenty-five pupils have received mentoring support from the community mentoring project and the LM has worked with fourteen mentor youth workers from the project.

The girls choose whether or not they want mentoring and the LM and youth service work together to match the girls with suitable community mentors. Each girl meets with her community mentor once a week. The relationship is needs led and can last up to a year. The LM has oversight of the project and ensures that the pupils are happy with the service they are receiving.

One community mentor helped one young woman with learning and emotional needs to make the transition to a further education college. She continued to meet with her community mentor for some time after she began college and the support gave her the confidence to make a success of her transition.

The girls on the community mentoring programme also have access to a variety of youth service programmes, such as youth clubs and the annual summer university. Access to the youth service programmes encourages active citizenship as they offer opportunities for involvement in community activities.

The girls who benefit from the community mentoring project evaluate it each year. The LM also requests formal, confidential, feedback from each community mentor. One girl wrote about her experience of the programme: 'Working with [my mentor] has opened a pathway to realising who I am.' Another wrote: 'Mentoring helped me to deal with problems that I could not handle or sort out by myself... It also taught me that the best way to deal with my problems was to be assertive and not aggressive.'

By working in partnership with the statutory youth service to deliver a mentoring scheme with a community focus, the learning mentor can offer a greater range of mentoring in the school.

Case study 33 explores a similar theme: the learning mentors from two schools in similar circumstances worked together, to the benefit of both schools and both communities. It also relates to case study 16 (p155) where learning mentors worked with each other to facilitate better outcomes for pupils.

Case study 33: Learning mentors at Seven Sisters Primary School and Downhills Primary School working together

The LMs in two Haringey primary schools put together a ten-week programme for five children in each school who were experiencing significant social, emotional and behavioural barriers to learning and participation. The final target was two day-trips – one to London and one to Paris. The project aimed to build up and secure relationships between the two recently amalgamated schools, develop children's social, emotional and behavioural skills, and build relationships with families. The LMs from both schools work with individuals from outside the school, particularly teachers at the City Learning Centre, a secondary school teacher and the School's Trip's Agency.

The project included lessons in French from a secondary school teacher, ICT research conducted at school and at the

City Learning Centre and the two whole day events – a trip to London and another to Paris. Thus the programme sought to develop language skills, ICT skills, social skills and engagement in the learning process. The children had a unique opportunity to research and learn about another language, country and culture. This – and the trips – enabled them to broaden their minds and their life experiences, as many of the children did not own a passport and had never travelled outside the UK.

The children acquired a good understanding of distance, travel and geography. They learned about currency, using maps, different foods, culture and languages. They were able to share their ideas and knowledge with each other, and to learn how to work together as a team. They developed confidence using PowerPoint and presenting and sharing their experiences during school assemblies.

Successful partnerships between families and the schools helped to increase parental involvement in the children's learning and raise their expectations of their children and the schools. The LMs and the families worked together to complete the travel form, think about and plan for safety issues and communicate with the school and authorities about the trips. The trusting and respectful relationships that developed between the families and the LMs meant that parents felt they could discuss other issues concerning school with the LMs.

This was the first time Haringey primary schools took pupils abroad. The LMs successfully tested the borough's new policy and procedures for educational visits.

The project proved to be a motivational tool for learning. The LMs' careful planning and well-placed trust in the children resulted in very successful trips and the children did their respective schools proud.

These learning mentors used their partnership to engage families and build a sense of community in the two recently amalgamated schools. They created an opportunity for a group of disenfranchised children to take school trips that facilitated good formal learning opportunities, but also helped them to establish a connection to their community and their city.

Case study 33 is a model of task-focused collaboration. The learning mentors worked together in collegial ways to reflect on their practice in a joint undertaking 'informed by the ideals and aspirations of collective practice infused by value rationality and the commitment to valued social ends' (Fielding, 1999:17).

Reflecting on practice

Learning mentors meet in local networks that are usually arranged by a co-ordinator in the local education authority but sometimes by a learning mentor in the practice community. Through these networks, learning mentors share effective practice with their colleagues, so enhancing local learning mentor provision. The learning mentor at Norlington School implemented Talk Time for Parents, inspired by the learning mentor at Sybourn Junior's account of her Talk Time approach at a network meeting. Opportunities for sharing effective practice are important, and so is engaging critically in reflective practice.

The *Value Base* (published alongside the *National Occupational Standards for Learning, Development and Support Services*) defines reflective practice as follows:

> A key aspect of professional practice is a reflection of practitioners' own contribution to the quality of service provision. Included in this is the expectation that practitioners will seek the views of service users (children, young people and their families/carers) and use them to inform and improve service delivery. Practitioners must compile a reflective practice log to demonstrate their commitment to being a reflective practitioner. A key aspect of being a reflective practitioner is a commitment to engaging in and encouraging others to participate in appropriate continuous professional development. (PAULO, ENTO and TOPSS, 2003b: 1)

Increasingly, learning mentors are involved in schools' performance management arrangements and have the opportunity to review their own practice through performance review or appraisal and to evaluate learning mentor provision by contributing to the annual cycle of school reporting and improvement planning. Many learning mentors undertake annual reviews of learning mentor provision alongside their line managers, identifying areas for development which are included in the school's improvement plan. A key part of reviewing learning mentor provision is seeking the views of the pupils and their families about improvement and act accordingly. In the Compact Club case study (p187), part of the way that the learning mentor evaluates the impact of the programme is through the pupils' views, and in case study 15 (p147-8) the learning mentor improves the stress management and study skills programme based on pupils' evaluations.

Performance management and reviewing learning mentor provision are valuable ways of reflecting on practice, but there is more to engaging critically in reflective practice. The *Value Base* suggests that learning mentors keep a 'reflective practice log' and it is a requirement for learning mentors undertaking the national vocational qualifications in Learning, Development and Support Services. But although important, a reflective practice log will not overcome what Colley (2003: 173) calls as 'the atomising effects of individual mentoring'.

While 'making use of supervision' is one of the suite of sixty-one units of competence in the *National Occupational Standards for Learning, Development and Support Services*, it is not compulsory. One-to-one professional supervision for learning mentors would require funding not currently available to schools. It is also unclear whether this would be desirable. According to Colley:

> Those involved in mentoring need to set aside time to reflect on what is happening in mentor relationships and in the settings which create them. Such reflection may be more effective if it is undertaken as a collective process within supportive networks... rather than as 'private affair that is about survival' (Issitt, 2000: 131). (Colley, 2003: 173)

Case study 34 documents how one group of learning mentors has piloted a peer supervision approach to help them engage critically in reflective practice.

Case study 34: Peervision in Waltham Forest – the power of peer learning

The pilot peervision group consists of four practising LMs in the secondary sector and the EIC Co-ordinator for LMs. All attended an initial one-day training session, sourced through Liverpool University and delivered by an experienced clinical supervisor. The training was based on materials from a clinical supervisors' course offered by the Centre Training School of Hypnotherapy and Psychotherapy.

Peervision is peer-based group supervision defined in the pilot as a working alliance among LMs in which each LM can reflect on her working environment by giving an account of work and receiving feedback, guidance and support if needed. The primary objective of this alliance is to maximise the competence and effectiveness of LMs in providing a helping service to young people.

The peervision group met five times in five months, for about an hour and half each time. A different member of the group facilitated each meeting, practicing her facilitation skills. Any notion of an 'expert' supervisor was rejected. At the start of each meeting, the facilitator asks if anyone has a case to bring and time is allocated accordingly.

Key objectives of peervision are:

- keeping children and young people's interests at the centre of learning mentoring
- sharing responsibility, practice and experience
- generating greater insight
- considering options, exploring difficulties, uncovering blind spots and challenging blockages and barriers
- developing alternative strategies
- avoiding isolation and offering reassurance
- developing and extending LM practice
- considering ethics and boundaries

The initial training used the supervision matrix developed by Hawkins and Shohet, which outlines six modes of supervision as a framework for peervision:

- reflection on the content of the mentoring session
- exploration of the strategies and interventions used by the LM
- exploration of the mentoring process
- focus on the LM's counter-transference
- focus on the here and now supervisory session
- focus on the facilitator's counter-transference.

In evaluating this model, the members of the peervision pilot group found the first three modes and a reframed fourth mode most useful. A case-centred, interactive approach was found most effective, focusing on reflection on the mentoring session, the strategies and interventions used by the LM, exploration of the mentoring process and relationship, and an opportunity for the group to explore any hidden dynamics.

The last three modes, focusing on counter-transference, are appropriate for clinical counselling practice but not, it was felt, for LM practice. This mismatch between the clinical nature of the model and the needs of the group was indicative of the tension between counselling and LM practice. This needs further consideration in terms of constructing an ethics of LM practice.

All the members have been committed to the group and no-one missed a meeting. They noted how they benefited: the group creates a safe space to speak about and reflect on cases, think of new strategies, identify moments of blindness and re-energise or re-engage with a case – it has developed and extended practice and provided greater insight into certain cases. Confidence and trust was rapidly established in the first meetings. The LMs can reflect on the tensions they may feel between the requirements of the school as an institution, and the need to keep the young people's interests at the centre of mentoring. And thanks to the group, they don't feel isolated in their school.

The intension is that peervision will be introduced in the secondary sector. LMs will be invited to attend peervision groups, and group membership will be closed. After a period of evaluation the primary sector will follow. The LMs who received the training in the original peervision group will act as facilitators to another group. The original group will continue to meet to offer peer based supervision to each other and to assure quality.

A published code of practice supports the process. It sets out a rationale for peervision, including its aims and objectives, key roles and responsibilities, the operational processes, confidentiality and accountability, and a procedure for quality assurance, monitoring and reviewing peervision groups. The code of practice offers guidance on bringing cases to supervision, including:

- how to manage, organise and present case material clearly

- how to recognise appropriate cases and aspects of work to discuss, including difficult or uncomfortable practice and cases

- the proportion and balance of cases to be discussed

- how to prioritise and make best use of time.

In their one-to-one work with young people, learning mentor practice must be both effective and safe. Peervision is a key component of safe and effective practice that supports and complements school-based line management. It is also a forum in which the norms and values of collective practice are negotiated. In Fielding's view, this qualifies as 'collegiality': practice that is 'intentionally and demonstrably linked to the furtherance of democracy' (1999: 17). Peervision seeks to constitute a 'communal practice in which colleagues' commitment to support one another is informed by their respect for professional expertise articulated and exemplified within the shared goals, values and practices of the profession' (Fielding, 1999: 18).

Case study 35 describes a different model of group supervision using a multi-agency approach and focused specifically on pupils' mental health.

> ### Case study 35: multi-agency group supervision for learning mentors in Camden
>
> The LM strand co-ordinator in Camden LEA worked with the co-ordinator for training at the local NHS institution for mental health care to see whether an experiential workshop series for LMs could be provided that would serve as a model of group supervision. The project would provide a forum for LMs to discuss and engage with the mental health issues affecting pupils and help them understand when and how to enable pupils to access the appropriate help.
>
> Eight ninety-minute sessions were to be provided for up to twenty LMs and be facilitated by a clinical psychologist and an educational psychologist. Costs would be split between the individual contributing schools and the Excellence in Cities central budget.
>
> Senior managers in schools were consulted by letter and at the termly line managers' forum. It was agreed that the project should go ahead as a pilot. The LM co-ordinator, the clinical psychologist and the educational psychologist planned the overall sessions and discussed a team strategy.
>
> The project was advertised in the local LMs' professional development programme and at local LM network meetings. LMs were invited to apply directly to the mental health care service, as the provider. Fifteen LMs across primary and secondary sectors signed up.
>
> LMs found the project of great value, as it has created an interactive space for them to reflect on their practice – both on specific cases and in general – in a shared but safe environment. They welcomed the sessions at the mental health care institute, away from the distractions of their workplaces. Participants gained access to professional information on specific mental health issues. The process of reflection and the information imparted on how to recognise and appropriately refer pupils with mental health issues was instantly transferable to their practice. Those who attended more than half of the ses

sions received qualifying certificates from the mental health care institute plus a year's access to the institute's library.

Following the evaluation of the pilot, it was decided to include more information on specific mental health issues and to restrict each group to between eight and ten participants. The evaluation also revealed that line managers of LMs needed access to specific training. Three twilight seminars were planned for school-based managers as well as lead LMs. Each seminar focused on specific issues, for instance the factors affecting risk-taking behaviour in children with mental health issues. Running them jointly with a neighbouring borough helped to fund expert speakers.

The take-up of the supervision workshops continues to be high.

This model situates collegiality and peer learning within a multi-agency context. It creates the opportunity for learning mentors to have a better understanding of mental health and also for mental health practitioners to engage with front-line professionals. The model of collegiate learning is transitive in its operation and effects. Engaging critically in reflective practice is crucial if learning mentor practice is to be safe, effective and have valued social ends. Opportunities for collegiate reflection need to be built into the structures within which learning mentors operate.

All 35 case studies map a complex practice field. In immersing ourselves in the particular, we seek the invariant: practice-based evidence that supports an emerging model of practice that is linked 'intentionally and demonstrably to the furtherance of democracy' (Fielding, 1999: 17).

Parting thoughts: seizing opportunities in a climate of possibility

The ending of Excellence in Cities as a grant-funded programme leaves programme managers and the practice community anxious and uncertain. But there is now a possibility of learning mentor practice becoming mainstream. It is time to move towards a conceptualisation of excellence that includes making schools more equitable. The unique contribution skilled learning mentors make to schools has been in bringing 'excellence in living' to many of the pupils they work with, but they cannot do this on their own. While schools can adjust positively to the new practices of learning mentors, it is for school leaders actively to transform their schools.

Transforming schools

The policy context offers possibilities. I recently heard a deputy head teacher say that it 'feels like the grip is beginning to loosen' and it may become possible to provide a more democratic education. The opportunity to promote and sustain the work of learning mentors should not be lost, now that its benefits to pupils and to schools are so evident.

What would a transformed school look like? It would be an inclusive environment in which all pupils were engaged and learned effectively. Its success would be judged on its pupils' learning, participation and continued capacity for growth. All

201

this is in line with the government's 'Building Schools for the Future' programme and the new duties on schools under *Every Child Matters.*

Fielding argues for schools that are transformed in terms of person-centred education and civic renewal. Schools that see pupils as partners in school improvement and change, operating in person-centred mode

> ...will be explicitly and engagingly mutual in [their] orientation towards widely conceived educational ends that will often include measurable results, but are not constituted or constrained by them. It is about students and teachers working and learning together in partnership, rather than one party using the other often for covert ends. Its processes and procedures are emergent, rather than fixed, and shaped by the dialogic values that underpin its aspirations and dispositions. (Fielding, 2004: 18)

Fielding echoes Rogers and Freiberg's call for schools to be active learning communities. They complain that schools still operate like factories and are built like boxes. They offer suggestions for how schools might be reformed, but it is their questions that are most interesting:

- How do we radically and permanently change the patterns of interactions between students and teachers to improve the capacity and joy of a child's learning?

- What support efforts are needed to create meaningful learning communities?

- How does the box known as school become transformed to respond to the needs of the person? (Rogers and Freiberg, 1994: 334)

I leave you with these questions and the idea that the work of learning mentors allows us to see the purpose of schooling differently. As this book has shown, learning mentors indubitably have a unique and valuable role in the transformation of schools.

Appendix A
Learning mentors supporting the five Every Child Matters Outcomes

Every Child Matters outcomes	Examples of how LMs support the outcomes. They	Page reference
1. Be healthy	run breakfast clubs	126,129,145,163
	various after-school clubs including sports and dance	144-147
	support schools to achieve the Healthy School Standard	140
	offer sex and relationship guidance	64,190
	support pupils with mental health issues	189-190
	support pupils to cope with bereavement and loss	178
	support pupils to find ways of coping with relationship difficulties	128-129,145-146,175-177, 178-179,184
	help build pupils' resilience	100,105,140
	make multi-agency links (CAMHS, EWS, health, Social Services)	164,184,189-190,199-200
2. Stay safe	operate bullying prevention programmes and strategies	134-140
	encourage and model positive play – including peaceful playground projects	130-134
	help pupils make positive choices re sex and relationships	64,190
	do child protection work	161,189-190
	family liaison	183-186

Every Child Matters outcomes	Examples of how LMs support the outcomes. They	Page reference
	make referrals to external agencies and multi-agency support (EWS, Youth Offending Teams, Social Services, Police, Tier one, two and three health and social care providers, community and voluntary sector organisations)	125-126, 147-148, 161, 164, 184, 189-190
3. Enjoy and achieve	support engagement with school and learning	124-147
	work with EWS to support attendance	124-127
	provide programmes to support personal and social development	128-129, 131, 132-133, 135-139, 142-143, 145-146
	provide study support and study skills programmes	147-148, 187-190
	work with families and carers including in family learning programmes	183-186
	support learning and participation through one-to-one and group work	112-118, 128-130, 175-177, 187-189
	run homework clubs	144-147, 187-190
4. Make a positive contribution	work with student councils	64
	provide peer support programmes (peer mentoring and peer buddying)	131-132, 140-144, 173
	provide programmes to enable pupils to support the environment and their communities (e.g. Princes Trust and award schemes)	128-129, 187-188
	support transfer and transition	152-165
	provide programmes to develop confidence and self-esteem	128-129, 135-139, 143-144, 175-177
	provide programmes to support social and emotional development	135-139, 142, 145-146
5. Achieve economic well-being	provide programmes to help pupils prepare for further education and employment	147-148, 187-188
	raise motivation and aspirations	187-188
	provide study support programmes that enhance exam success	147-148
	plan for progression	188

References

Apple, M. (1990) *Ideology and the Curriculum*, London: Routledge

Aronowitz, S. and Giroux, H. (1991) *Postmodern Education: politics, culture and social criticism*, Minneapolis: University of Minnesota Press

Association for Child and Youth Care Practice (2002) North American Certification Project: competencies for professional child and youth work practitioners, *Journal of Child and Youth Care Work*, 17, 16-49

Baker, J. (2003) *Primary Peer Buddying Programme: Training Materials*, Sheffield: Education Directorate

Bayley, J. and Haddock, L. (1999) *Training Teachers in Behaviour Management.* London: SENJIT

Blake, W. (1979) *Blake's Poetry and Designs*, edited by Johnson, M and Grant, J. New York: W.W. Norton

Boal, A. (1998) *Legislative Theatre: Using performance to make politics*, London: Routledge

Booth, T. (1997) Mapping Inclusion and Exclusion: Concepts for All? In Clark, C. Dyson, A. and Millward, A. (eds) *Towards Inclusive Schools?* London: David Fulton

Bourdieu, P. and Passerson, J. (1970) *Reproduction in Education and Society*, London: Sage

Bradford, S. (2000) Disciplining practices: new ways of making youth workers accountable, *International Journal of Adolescence and Youth*, 9, 45-63

Brendtro, L. Brokenleg, M and Van Bockern, S. (1990) *Reclaiming Youth at Risk: Our Hope for the Future*, Indiana: Bloomington

Brendtro, L. and Ness, A. (1983) *Re-educating Troubled Youth*, New York: Aldine De Gruyter

Bronfenbrenner, U. (1979) *The Ecology of Human Development: Experiments by nature and design*, Harvard University Press

Brown, D. (2004) *Bullying: from reaction to prevention*, Surrey: Young Voice

Cannan, C. and Warren, C. (1997) *Social Action with Children and Families: A community development approach to child and family welfare*, London: Routledge

Centre for Studies in Inclusive Education (2000) *Index for Inclusion: developing learning and participation in schools.* Bristol: CSIE

Colley, H. (2003) *Mentoring for Social Inclusion: a critical approach to nurturing mentoring relationships,* London: RoutledgeFalmer

Commission for Race Equality (CRE) (2001) *Statutory code of practice on the duty to promote Race Equality: a guide for schools,* Norwich, CRE Publications

Cruddas, L. and Haddock, L. (2003) *Girls' Voices: Supporting girls' learning and emotional development,* Stoke on Trent: Trentham

Daniels, H. (2001) *Vygotsky and Pedagogy,* London: RoutledgeFalmer

Dewey, J. (1916) *Democracy and Education,* London: Kessinger

DfEE (1997) *Excellence for all Children – meeting special educational needs,* Nottingham: DfEE Publications

DfEE (1999a) *Excellence in Cities,* Nottingham: DfEE Publications

DfEE (1999b) *Social Inclusion: pupil support* (Circular 10/99), London: The Stationery Office

DfES (2001) *Inclusive Schooling: Children with special educational needs,* Nottingham: DfES Publications

DfES (2002) *Bullying: Don't Suffer in Silence – an anti-bullying pack for schools,* Nottingham: DfES Publications

DfES (2003a) *Aiming Higher: Raising the Achievement of Gypsy Traveller Pupils,* Nottingham: DfES Publications

DfES (2003b) *Every Child Matters* (Green Paper), Norwich: The Stationery Office

DfES (2003c) *Managing Pupil Mobility: Guidance,* Nottingham: DfES Publications

DfES (2003d) *The Learning Challenge: Handbook for school organisers,* Nottingham: DfES Publications

DfES (2004a) *Common Assessment Framework Consultation Document,* http://www.dfes.gov.uk/consultations/downloadableDocs/ACF006.pdf

DfES (2004b) *EIC Overview,* http://www.standards.dfes.gov.uk/sie/eic/EICoverview

DfES (2004c) *Excellence in Cities: Progress to Date,* http://www.standards.dfes.gov.uk/sie/document/EICProgress.doc

DfES (2004d) *Every Child Matters: Next Steps,* Norwich: The Stationery Office

DfES (2004e) *Every Child Matters: Change for Children,* Norwich: The Stationery Office

DfES (2004f) *Five Year Strategy for Children and Learners: Putting people at the heart of public services,* Norwich: The Stationery Office

Dobson, J. Henthorne, K. and Lynas, Z. (2000) *Pupil Mobility in Schools: Final Report,* Migration Research Unit: University of London

Egan, G. (2002) *The Skilled Helper: a problem-management and opportunity-development approach to helping,* California: Brooks/Cole

ENTO, PAULO and TOPSS (2003a) *National Occupational Standards for Learning, Development and Support Services for children, young people and those who care for them*, online, http://www.dfes.gov.uk/childrenandfamilies/docs/qualification_structure.pdf

ENTO, PAULO and TOPSS (2003b) *Value Base: National Occupational Standards for Learning, Development and Support Services for children, young people and those who care for them*, http://www.dfes.gov.uk/childrenandfamilies/docs/value_base.pdf

Fewster, G. (2002) Growing Together: the personal relationship in child and youth care, *Journal of Child and Youth Care*, 15(4), 5-16

Fielding, M. (1999) *Radical Collegiality: Affirming teaching as an Inclusive Professional Practice*, http://www.sussex.ac.uk/education/documents/radical 2.pdf

Fielding, M. (2004) 'New Wave' Student Voice and the Renewal of Civic Society, *London Review of Education*, 2(3), 197-217

Fullan, M. (2003) *The Moral Imperative of School Leadership*, California: Corwin Press

Galton, M and MacBeath, J. (2002) *A Life in Teaching: Impact of change of primary teachers' working lives*, London: National Union of Teachers

Galton, M. Gray, J. and Ruddock, J. (1999) *The Impact of School Transitions and Transfers on Pupil Progress and Attainment* (DfEE Research Report RR131), Nottingham: DfEE Publications

Gilborn, D. and Mirza, H. (2000) *Educational Inequality: Mapping Race, Class and Gender*, Ofsted Publications Office

Gee, J. (1990) *Social Linguistics and Literacies: Ideology in discourses*, London: Falmer

Grey, C. (2001) *Against Learning* (Research Papers in Management Studies), Cambridge: Judge Institute of Management

Henderson, N. and Milstein, M. (2003) *Resiliency in Schools: Making it happen for students and educators*, California: Corwin

Lave, J. and Wenger, E. (1991) *Situated Learning: legitimate peripheral participation*, Cambridge: Cambridge University Press

Law, S. (2000) *The Philosophy Files*, London: Orion

Leadbeater, C. (2004) *Learning about Personalisation: how can we put the learner at the heart of the education system?* Nottingham: DfES Publications

Marshall, W. (1996) *Professionals, children and power. Exclusion from School: inter-professional issues for policy and practice*. Blyth, E. and Milner, J. (Eds). London: Routledge

Milliband, D. (2004) *Choice and Voice in Personalised Learning*, http://www.dfes.gov.uk/speeches/media/documents/PLfinal.doc

Morris, M. Rutt, S. and Eggers, A. (2004a) *Pupil Outcomes: The impact of EIC*, http://www.nfer.ac.uk/research/documents/EIC/Pupilout.doc

Morris, M. and Rutt, S. (2004b) *Analysis of Pupil Attendance: Data in Excellence in Cities Areas – an Interim Report* (DfES Research Report RR571), Nottingham: DfES Publications Centre

Organisation for Economic Co-operation and Development (OECD) (2001) *Executive Summary: Knowledge and Skills for Life: first results from the OECD programme for international student assessment* (PISA) 2000, http://www.pisa.oecd.org/dataoecd/44/53/33691596.pdf

Office for Standards in Education (Ofsted) (1999) *Raising the Attainment of Minority Ethnic Pupils – School and LEA Responses*, Ofsted

Ofsted (2002) *Changing Schools: An evaluation of the effectiveness of transfer arrangements at age 11*, Ofsted

Ofsted (2003a) *Excellence in Cities and Education Action Zones: management and impact*, Ofsted

Ofsted (2003b) *Framework for Inspecting Schools*, Ofsted

Ofsted (2005) *Framework for Inspecting Schools*,Ofsted

Piore, M. and Sabel, C. (1986) *The Second Industrial Divide: possibilities for prosperity*, Basic Books

Robinson, K., (2001) *All Our Futures: Creativity, Culture and Education. National Advisory Committee on Creative and Cultural Education.* London: The Stationery Office

Rogers, C. and Freiberg, J. (1994) *The Freedom to Learn*, New Jersey: Prentice Hall

Sauvé Bell Associates (2003) *Functional Map for the Provision of Learning Mentor Services*, www.paulo.org.uk/pages/nos/funct_map_Learn03.doc

Smith, M. (1999) *Social Pedagogy*, www.infed.org/biblio/b-socped.htm

Spafford, T. and Bolloton, B. (2004) Unpublished Training Materials, www.refugeeeducation.co.uk

Teare, B. (1997) *Effective Provision for Able and Talented Children*, Network Educational Press

UNESCO (1994) *Salamanca Statement and Framework for Action on special needs education*, http://www.unesco.org/education/pdf/SALAMA_E.pdf

Vitler, K. (2002) Social Pedagogy: what's in it for us? www.childrenuk.co.uk/chjul2002/chjul2002/social percent20ped.html

Vygotsky, L. (1978) *Mind in Society: the development of higher psychological processes*, M. Cole, V. John-Steiner, S. Scribner, and E. Souberman (eds and trans.), Cambridge: Harvard University Press

Wilms, J. (2003) *Student Engagement at School: A sense of belonging and participation – Results from PISA 2000*, OECD report, http://www.pisa/oecd.org/dataoecd/42/35/33689437.pdf

Winstanley, C. (2004) *Too Clever by Half – a fair deal for gifted children*, Stoke on Trent: Trentham

Index

achievement
and academic
mentoring 115-
117
and transfer 152
gap between
highest and lowest
35-38, 49, 67, 103
LMs' contribution
to 2, 38-40, 147-
148, 177, 179-180,
187-189
relationship to
engagement 43
action planning 68, 80,
82, 117-120, 121,
124, 126, 142, 184,
189
Aronowitz and Giroux
3, 81
assessment 68, 89-90,
114, 118-124, 147,
151, 165, 184
see also common
assessment
attendance 16, 64, 66
and engagement
124-125
interventions to
support 123-127,
146
relationship to
attainment 44, 68,
125

Baker 141-143
barriers to learning and
participation 52-
59, 67, 75, 84, 104,
120, 151, 163, 174,
179, 184
school-based 130-
134
Bayley and Haddock
90, 174
behaviour 89-90, 107,
114, 123, 128-129,
131, 142, 163, 168,
169, 175-177
behaviour
improvement
programme 20
belonging 9, 18, 35, 42-
43, 58, 59, 76, 99,
102
interventions to
support 124-127,
128-130, 131-134,
135-139, 187-189
bereavement 178
Booth 42
breakfast clubs 76, 126,
129, 145, 163-164,
see also clubs
Brendtro, Brokenleg
and Van Bockern
102, 130
Brendtro and Ness 87-
92
Bronfenbrenner 54-59,
75, 93

Brown 134
bullying prevention,
143, 175, 178-179,
134-140

Cannan and Warren 24,
26
Centre for Studies in
Inclusive
Education 52
child and youth care
26-33, 84, 87-89
American
Association for 26
definition of 26
NACP 26-33
competence links
with LMs 29-32
Children Act (2004) 17,
20, 28
children's
commissioner 28
children's services 19,
26
children's workforce 33,
69, 75
Children's Workforce
Unit 20
circle of courage 102,
130, 139, 189
circle time 63, 145-146,
176
City Learning Centre
64, 158, 192-193
clubs 144-147, 176 *see
also* compact club

209

cohorts – identifying
59-60
collaboration between
LMs16, 155-156,
192 see also multi-
agency working
Colley 2, 11,23,37, 38,
50, 74, 83, 98, 99,
111, 127, 195
common assessment
20 see also
assessment
Common
Assessment
Framework 120,
121
community education
25, 146
community mentoring
186, 191-192
compact club 187-189
comprehensive
education 47-49
Connexions 21, 25, 42,
73, 79
personal advisors
21, 24
creativity 63, 154-160,
171, 173, 179-183

Daniels 8, 11, 25, 56-57,
85, 87, 92, 101, 159
data collection see
monitoring and
evaluation
democracy 84-85, 93,
103-108
Dewey 8, 24, 84-85, 101,
103, 134, 144
digital video 63
discourse see learning
discourses
discourse guides 11,
101, 173
DfES 5 year strategy 21
Dobson 166
drama see learning,
drama as a tool for

ecological systems
theory 54-59, 75-
76, 83, 89, 93, 118-
124, 160
see also
assessment
economic well-being
see Every Child
Matters outcomes
educational visits 187-
189, 192-193
education welfare
officers/service 21,
24, 64, 68, 73, 79,
125-126
Egan 56, 75-76, 84, 87,
88-89, 91, 93-100,
112-114, 115-118,
122, 126, 129, 139,
149, 167
and action
planning 118-120
three stage
helping model
115-118
emancipatory theory 1,
3-6, 81
emotional and
behavioural
difficulties 53-54
and SEN 54
see also behaviour
emotional intelligence
3, 138
empathy 96-97, 136
see also values
empowerment 95, 98-
99, 101-103, 117,
127, 136, 175, 185
see also values
engagement 6, 45-46
39-50, 60
and attendance
124-125
and belonging 43
and participation
43
interventions to
support 124-147
relationship to
achievement 43

relationship to
transfer 152-154,
158-159
enjoy and achieve see
Every Child
Matters outcomes
enrichment activities
see extended
services
equality and diversity
46, 51-52, 60, 96,
103-108, 120, 128,
134, 169-170, 173
Every Child Matters
Change for
Children 19
Green Paper 19,
21, 28
integration of
services 19
outcomes 19, 43,
46, 66, 112, 124,
130, 154, 174, 188,
190, 202
Excellence in Cities
aims of 15
and inclusion 42
excellence clusters
16
funding 18
primary extension
16
re-engineering of
17-18
success of 17
exclusion 37, 42, 98,
114, 116
exclusionary
pressures 57, 76
managing the risk
of 124, 128-130,
158-159
extended schools 20,
66, 68-69, 189-190

families see parents and
families
Fewster 97
Fielding 1-2, 8, 10, 22,
189, 200, 202

freedom to learn 104
Freire 24
friendships 40, 145-146, 161, 178
Fullan 6, 10, 18, 35, 38, 48, 49
functional map 16, 73-82, 107-108, 111, 118, 151, 183, 186
functional definition of learning
mentoring 16, 73-82, 83
funding *see* Excellence in Cities

Galton 152-154, 158
Galton and Macbeath 154
Gee 4-5
gifted and talented 52, 140, 169-174
Gilborn and Mirza 37
goals 116-117, 118, 126, 127, 129-130, 149, 174
Grey 2, 7
group work 63, 128-130, 135-140, 175-177, 187-189
Gypsy Traveller children *see* Traveller children

healthy schools 140
Henderson and Milstein 105
humanism/humanistic teaching 90-91

ICT 158, 168, 173, 193
inclusion 2, 9, 41, 42, 46, 130, 134, 141, 182
definition of 42, 45
guidance:
leadership and management of 51
register 59
Index for Inclusion 52

inequality 45, 57-49
and achievement 35-38
and attendance 125-127
inspection *see* Ofsted
institutional barriers 76
instrumentalist model *see* learning discourses
intimate consultation *see* personalised learning

Lave and Wenger 8, 87
Leadbeater 22, 162
leadership 33, 35-50, 69
learning
as a site of struggle 10
as social practice 3, 81, 100-101, 134, 174
difficulties/ disabilities 57
discourses/ models of 2, 7-9, 10, 70, 86, 101
drama as a tool for 175-177, 184
facilitators of 8
in personal growth 112
instrumentalist model 7
programmes to enhance the joy of 169, 179-182
pupil management of 153-154, 159
styles 22, 79-80
transitive model 8-9, 10
looked after children 161-162

management
of LMs 51-70
mental health 199-200

mentoring
models of 23
functions 74
mid-term admissions *see* mobility
Milliband 21, 47
minister for children, young people and families 28
mobility 160, 165-168
DfES guidance 165
monitoring
and evaluation 61, 80
relation to under-achievement 60
moral imperative 6, 10, 18, 35-50, 134, 166
Morris and Rutt 44-45, 125
Morris, Rutt and Eggers 38-39, 45-46
motivation 63, 81, 117, 126
and transfer 152-154
programmes to support 124, 142, 144-147, 171, 177, 180, 187-189, 193
multi-agency working 20, 59, 69, 164, 184, 187-190, 198-200

National Occupational Standards 21, 24, 27-33, 195
and NACP 27-33
knowledge and understanding in 79-82
qualifications based on 27, 79
see also Value Base
networks 194 *see also* multi-agency working, reflection on practice and parents and families

neo-liberalism 1-3
new arrivals *see*
    mobility

OECD 36
Ofsted
    and *Every Child
    Matters* outcomes
    66-67
    comments on LM
    practice 17, 133,
    159, 164, 188
    framework for
    inspecting schools
    35, 38, 46, 51, 66,
    70
    preparing for
    inspections 62-67
    report on EIC 17
    report on transfer
    and transition 152

parents and families
    and assessment
    121, 123
    views of 61, 68
    work with 64-65,
    68, 76, 126, 137,
    163, 164, 165, 171,
    176, 178, 181-182,
    183-186, 189, 193
participation 9, 11, 16,
    22, 42-45, 51, 87,
    127
    barriers to
    learning 52-59
    interventions to
    increase 124-147
    in the working
    alliance 94, 100
pedagogy
    border 5
    definition of 25
peer buddies/mentors
    140-144
peer support *see*
    support
performance
    management 61,
    62, 194-195

personal growth and
    development 57,
    67, 84, 101-103,
    117, 164, 177
    and assessment
    121
    and transfer 154,
    159, 160, 162
personalised learning
    21, 22, 48, 78-79,
    162, 165, 179, 182
person centred
    practice10, 78-79,
    94-99
philosophy for children
    172-173
Piaget 92
PISA 36, 76, 169
playgrounds 76, 131,
    140, 164
    buddies 131, 164
    see also peer
    buddies
    overcoming
    barriers in 130-134
positive psychology 84,
    93, 113, 122
post-structuralism 1, 6-
    7, 8
power 4, 6, 89, 90, 99,
    126-127
    as social influence
    126-127
pragmaticism 91-92
preventative work 20,
    140
PSHE 64, 66
psychoeducational
    model 87-92, 93
pupil voice 61-62, 69,
    194
pyramid club 145-146
    see also clubs

qualifications *see*
    National
    Occupational
    Standards

race equality 167
    Race Relations
    (Amendment) Act
    2000 38, 41
reading, programmes
    179-182
reclaiming
    environments 102
    playgrounds 131
reflection
    on practice 61, 91,
    99, 194-200
    with young people
    101
refugees 166 *see also*
    mobility
relationships 88-89, 93,
    164, 167
    among peers 67,
    142, 178-179
    in facilitation of
    learning 77, 120,
    128, 145-146, 175-
    177
    see also working
    alliance
resilience 100, 105, 140
rights 80-82, 90, 172
risk 2, 105
Robinson *et al* 155-157,
    182
Rogers and Freiberg 77,
    78, 94, 97, 101-103,
    104, 106, 202

school improvement
    10, 17, 18, 35-50,
    52
    contribution of
    peer support to
    142-144, 174
    plans 62
school councils 64, 66,
    131
school self-evaluation
    46, 62
Schools Workforce Unit
    20
self-esteem 63, 80, 121,
    135, 142, 171, 175,
    188

self-referral 177-179
situated learning
    theory 9, 87
skilled helping *see* Egan
Smith 24, 25
social development
    theory 86, 92, 93
social inclusion *see*
    inclusion
social pedagogy 24, 25
    theories 84-87
solution focused
    therapies 118, 119
Spafford and Bolloten
    166-167
special educational
    needs 46, 52-54,
    125
    and Disability and
    Discrimination
    Act 41
    register 59
standards 10, 18, 70
story sacks 180
stress management
    147-149
study skills 116, 147-
    148
support
    and guidance 69,
    74
    definition of 52
    pastoral 169, 174-
    177
    peer 141, 166, 173
    see also peer
    buddies/ mentors
support groups 135-140
support staff 131, 132,
    163-164
    roles of 47, 53

targets *see* goals
teaching assistants 75
    see also support
    staff
Teare 160
thinking skills 172-173
transactional analysis
    90
transfer and transition
    63-64, 66, 143,
    151-165
    definitions of 152
    as a status passage
    159
Traveller children 166-
    167

underachievement 37,
    59-60, 171, 172,
    175, 186, 191
    at transfer 152

values 80, 85, 91, 94-99,
    128
Value Base 60, 94-95,
    96, 194, 195
Vygotsky 8, 85-87, 92,
    100, 104, 120, 143

Wilms 42-44
Winstanley 169
workforce reform 19, 20
working alliance 6, 67,
    86, 93-94, 100, 103,
    112, 120, 121, 122,
    127, 160, 172, 196
    definition 89, 93

Youth Service 190-192

zone of proximal
    development 86,
    100, 104
    see also Vygotsky